Thoughts and Dreams
of an Old Theologian

Thoughts and Dreams of an Old Theologian

LEONARDO BOFF

Translated by
Francis McDonagh

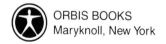

ORBIS BOOKS
Maryknoll, New York

Founded in 1970, Orbis Books endeavors to publish works that enlighten the mind, nourish the spirit, and challenge the conscience. The publishing arm of the Maryknoll Fathers and Brothers, Orbis seeks to explore the global dimensions of the Christian faith and mission, to invite dialogue with diverse cultures and religious traditions, and to serve the cause of reconciliation and peace. The books published reflect the views of their authors and do not represent the official position of the Maryknoll Society. To learn more about Maryknoll and Orbis Books, please visit our website at www.orbisbooks.com

English translation copyright © 2022 by Orbis Books
Original title: *Reflexões de um velho teólogo e pensador*, copyright © 2020 (Petropolis, Brazil: Editora Vozes).
English translation published by Orbis Books, Box 302, Maryknoll, NY 10545–0302.
Manufactured in the United States of America

Library of Congress Cataloging-in-Publication Data

Names: Boff, Leonardo, author. | McDonagh, Francis, translator.
Title: Thoughts and dreams of an old theologian / Leonardo Boff ; translated by Francis McDonagh.
Other titles: Reflexões de um velho teólogo e pensador. English
Description: Maryknoll, NY : Orbis Books, [2022] | Originally published: Reflexões de um velho teólogo e pensador. Petrópolis: Editora Vozes, 2018. | Includes bibliographical references and indexes. | Summary: "Brazilian theologian Leonardo Boff, a pioneer of liberation theology, reviews the major themes of his work, including God, Christ, Ecology, Ethics, and Spirituality" — Provided by publisher.
Identifiers: LCCN 2021043125 (print) | LCCN 2021043126 (ebook) | ISBN 9781626984547 (print) | ISBN 9781608339174 (ebook)
Subjects: LCSH: Boff, Leonardo. | Liberation theology.
Classification: LCC BX4705.B545 A3 2022 (print) | LCC BX4705.B545 (ebook)
  | DDC 230/.2 — dc23/eng/20211015
LC record available at https://lccn.loc.gov/2021043125
LC ebook record available at https://lccn.loc.gov/2021043126

Peregrinantibus mecum
To those who walked the road with me

Contents

Publisher's Note   ix

1. "I Have a Dream"   1

2. What Is This Creature That Thinks
   It Can Do Theology?   7

3. God, the Originating Principle of All Beings   22

4. The Son of the Father Is among Us:
   Jesus of Nazareth   36

5. The Holy Spirit, Giver of Life, and
   the Feminine Element   49

6. The Church: Charism and Power,
   and the People of God   59

7. Freeing Mother Earth: An Ecotheology
   of Liberation   79

8. An Ethics That Is Universal and for
   the Common Home   100

9. Spirituality, the Depths of a Human Being   142

Conclusion: A Minimal Spirituality
of Mother Earth   169

Selection of Works by Leonardo Boff   173

Publisher's Note

In a career spanning over fifty years, the Brazilian theologian and philosopher Leonardo Boff has been widely recognized as one of the most creative and prophetic figures of our time. Here, from the perspective of his eighties, he offers an overview of a body of work marked both by surprising lines of continuity and by ongoing renewal in light of the signs of the times.

Boff was born in Concordia, Brazil, in 1938, the eldest of eleven children. He joined the Franciscan order and was ordained a priest in 1964. After earning a doctorate in theology in Munich in 1971 he returned to Brazil, where he soon established himself as a prolific and influential author, publishing on a wide range of theological topics, as well as popular works on spirituality.

In the early 1970s, Boff, along with Gustavo Gutiérrez, Jon Sobrino, and Juan Luis Segundo, became known as one of the original pioneers of the emerging theology of liberation. That decade coincided with the origins of Orbis Books, the leading English-language publisher of Latin American theology, and thus it marked the beginning of our long and fruitful relationship with Leonardo Boff. His early Orbis titles included *Jesus Christ Liberator, Liberating Grace, Ecclesiogenesis: The Base Communities Reinvent the Church, Trinity and Society,* and, with his brother Clodovis, *Introducing Liberation Theology.* (See the list of Boff's English translations at the end of this book.)

Liberation theology undertook to survey all questions of faith from the perspective of the poor and oppressed. Among other things, this perspective brought to light certain features of the gospel—particularly Jesus's proclamation of "good news to the poor," his central message of the Kingdom of God, and his conflict with the ruling powers of his day that led to his death. As a Franciscan, Boff was especially attentive to the echoes between liberation theology and the way of St. Francis, who in an earlier age had made a radical option for the poor and marginalized. (See *Francis of Assisi: A Model of Human Liberation.*)

Liberation theology was not just a theme for academic study. It involved new pastoral strategies. It took root in a new ecclesial phenomenon, the "base Christian communities" that emerged among the rural and urban poor. In the context of oppressive military governments this "option for the poor" entailed profound risks. In the words of St. Óscar Romero, those who took the side of the poor risked "sharing the same fate as the poor," and it followed that many priests and religious, bishops, and countless lay faithful faced imprisonment, torture, and death.

But opposition also came from within the church. In the 1980s, liberation theology was scrutinized by the Vatican, which worried that this theology relied on Marxist analysis and risked division and politicization of the church. Leonardo Boff was singled out for special investigation by Cardinal Josef Ratzinger (later Pope Benedict XVI), prefect of the Congregation for the Doctrine of the Faith. The focus was Boff's work *Church: Charism and Power* (1981), which directed critical analysis to the structures of authority in the church itself.

In 1985, following a year of investigation, Boff was ordered to maintain a period of "obedient silence." Boff submitted to this instruction, explaining, "I would rather walk with the church than alone with my theology." Though the silencing was lifted after a year, he continued to face ongoing censorship and restrictions on his writings and teaching. As a result, in 1992, he announced his intention to leave the priesthood as well as his Franciscan community.

In a letter addressed to his "Companions on the Path of Hope," he described the external pressures that had made it increasingly difficult for him to continue his work as a theologian. As he wrote, "To be unfaithful to what gives sense to one's life is to lose one's dignity and to diminish one's identity. This I will not do, nor do I think that God wants this of us." Nevertheless, he took pains to stress that he was not leaving the church or abandoning his vocation as a theologian: "I continue to be and will always be a theologian in the Catholic and ecumenical mold, fighting with the poor against their poverty and in favor of their liberation."

In fact, this transition freed Boff to widen his field of reflection beyond narrowly theological topics. Increasingly he addressed social and ethical themes of global and planetary concern. In particular, Boff was among the first to incorporate a concern for ecology in the sphere of liberation theology. With the title of his landmark book *Cry of the Earth, Cry of the Poor,* he introduced a phrase later adopted by Pope Francis.

In many ways the election in 2013 of Pope Francis, the first pope from Latin America, represented a confirmation of many of Boff's long-running themes. Boff recognized in the pope's historic adoption of the name Francis a clear and deliberate statement of his agenda for the church. In *Francis of Assisi, Francis of Rome,* Boff elaborated on the Franciscan spirit evident in the pope's ideal of a "poor church for the poor," his call for ecological conversion, his emphasis on mercy, nonviolence, and the "joy of the gospel." Confirming this intuition, the pope's two major encyclicals, *Laudato Si': Care for Our Common Home,* and *Fratelli Tutti: Fraternity and Social Friendship,* both drew explicitly on a Franciscan reading of the gospel.

Boff's concerns in recent decades have taken him far beyond an exclusively Catholic audience. He has been a critical contributor to international forums on ecology and "earth ethics." In 2001 he received the "Right Livelihood Award"—sometimes dubbed the "alternative Nobel Prize." Through his writings on social issues, ethics, and the dialogue between religion and science, he has reached an international audience, and his works have appeared in many languages.

In the present work, which was commissioned by Boff's long-term Brazilian publisher Vozes, he offers a kind of summing-up of his thoughts as a now-"old theologian." Many of these thoughts were previewed or tested over the years in his previous publications with Orbis Books, but it is helpful to see them in the context of his growth and development as both a "thinker" and a "dreamer."

In one of his more recent books, he took stock of his career in these words: "When people ask me: 'What are you doing in life?' I answer: 'I am a worker like any other, like a carpenter or an electrician. Only my instruments are very subtle: only twenty-six letters.'"[1]

Answering the question of what he tries to do with these letters, he responds:

> I just try to think, in tune, with the greatest concerns of human beings in the light of God; to arouse in them a confidence in the hidden potentialities within themselves to find solutions; to try to reach the hearts of people so that they have compassion for the unjust suffering of the world and of nature, so that they never desist from always improving reality, and so beginning to improve themselves. That way, regardless of their moral condition, they may always feel themselves

---

1. With Anselm Grün, *Becoming New: Finding God within Us and in Creation* (Maryknoll, NY: Orbis Books, 2019).

in the hand of God-Father-and-Mother of infinite kindness and mercy.

And so, after all, was it worth it? Here, he responds with the poet Fernando Pessoa: "'Everything is worth it if the soul is not small.' I have tried not to be small. I leave the last word to God. Now in the evening of life, I review the past days and my mind is turned toward eternity."

We are proud to have accompanied him thus far on this journey. We pray it will long continue.

Robert Ellsberg
Publisher, Orbis Books

1

"I Have a Dream"

These words of Martin Luther King Jr. (1929–1968), spoken some years before he was assassinated, come to my mind at this moment when I reach the age of eighty and have spent more than fifty years as a theologian. My eyes are fixed on my past, which I will be describing in this book, but my thoughts are directed at young people and my mind on eternity.

The Importance of Dreams

I attach great importance to dreams, those dreamed with closed eyes at night and with open eyes by day. The arguments of psychoanalysis, especially those of C. G. Jung, attach enormous importance to dreams, because they come from the deepest part of ourselves. A dream is the voice of the personal and collective unconscious, particularly the great dreams that have to do with our most radical identity and our life's destiny.

In the First and Second Testaments of the Bible, dreams are a way in which God communicates with his people, with the judges and the prophets. The patriarchs receive messages in dreams (Gen 15:12–21; 20:3–6; 28:11–22; 37:5–11; 46:4). The judges, who were popular leaders (Judg 2:16–19) and the kings (1 Kgs 3), and especially the prophets (1 Sam 3:2; 2 Sam 7:4–17; Zech 6:25; Dan 2:7; Joel 2:28), also received divine messages in dreams. I feel included in the words of the prophet Joel: "afterward your old men shall dream dreams, and your

1

young men shall see visions" (Joel 2:28; Acts 2:14–17). I hope very much that the young people who read this book will have hopeful visions for the future of life and of our Mother Earth, seriously threatened by aggression of all sorts caused by the irrationality of our civilization, which knows no limits and has no respect for any living creature.

In the Second Testament, Joseph, the husband of Mary and social father of Jesus, never uttered a word, but just had dreams (Matt 1–2). As a worker, he spoke with his calloused hands. Because of this he is the patron of anonymous workers, those who never get any publicity but live by gospel values. He was fundamental as a caring father and provider for the Holy Family: he protected his son from Herod's bloody plan by taking him into exile in Egypt. Saint Paul had dreams at night that showed him the way he should go (Acts 16:9–10; 18:9; 23:11; 27:23).

Israel's great dream was to possess a land flowing with milk and honey (Exod 3:15–18). No one less than the prophet Isaiah, in the second century BCE, launched a supreme dream:

> For I am about to create new heavens
>   and a new earth;
> the former things shall not be remembered
>   or come to mind.
> But be glad and rejoice forever
>   in what I am creating;
> for I am about to create Jerusalem as a joy,
>   and its people as a delight.
> I will rejoice in Jerusalem,
>   and delight in my people;
> no more shall the sound of weeping be heard in it,
>   or the cry of distress.
> No more shall there be in it
>   an infant that lives but a few days,
>   or an old person who does not live out a lifetime;

for one who dies at a hundred years will be
    considered a youth,
    and one who falls short of a hundred will be
    considered accursed.
They shall build houses and inhabit them;
    they shall plant vineyards and eat their fruit.
They shall not build and another inhabit;
    they shall not plant and another eat;
for like the days of a tree shall the days of my
    people be,
    and my chosen shall long enjoy the work of their
    hands.
They shall not labor in vain,
    or bear children for calamity;
for they shall be offspring blessed by the Lord —
    and their descendants as well.
Before they call I will answer,
    while they are yet speaking I will hear.
The wolf and the lamb shall feed together,
    the lion shall eat straw like the ox;
    but the serpent — its food shall be dust!
They shall not hurt or destroy
    on all my holy mountain. (Isa 65:17–25)

This dream is undying and, like any dream or utopia, in some way it anticipates the future that is to come.

Jesus's Undying Dream

The greatest dream of all is Jesus's, the Kingdom of God already present among us. The signs of its presence are the liberating acts of Jesus: healing the sick, cleansing a sufferer from Hansen's disease, restoring sight to the blind, raising his friend Lazarus from the dead, multiplying loaves and fishes for a starving crowd, calming the stormy waters of Lake Gennesaret and forgiving sins (Matt 8:3–27; Luke 7:48–

49). After this there will be release for captives and freedom for the oppressed (Luke 4:18-19), and a world will come in which the poor, the hungry and thirsty, those who weep and suffer, will be happy (Luke 6:20-21). Finally there will be "a new heaven and a new earth, and God himself will be with them; he will wipe every tear from their eyes. Death will be no more; mourning and crying and pain will be no more, for the first things have passed away" (Rev 21:1, 3-4).

Dreams as Nightmares

All peoples have their dreams that inspire them to work to make them come true. In modern times we have had and still have the dream of capitalism, of a society of plenty. It worked for a small group at the expense of two perverse injustices: the social injustice that left millions and millions poor and abandoned and the ecological disaster that has devastated nature. This dream, though it continues, is threatening the physiochemical and ecological underpinnings of life. The utopia of socialism wanted to create an equal society, but one imposed from above that erased each individual's identity. This dream cost the lives of millions and disappeared in history. But we have to nurture dreams if we are not to stagnate and get bogged down in the swamp created by the interests of powerful minorities that dominate the great mass of the people. Most of these huge dreams ended in a nightmare, that is to say, in dreams with bad consequences, especially for the poor and marginalized. Any nightmare comes from the unconscious, with images of tragic events, people attacking us, or life-threatening situations, frightening us and creating anxiety. Nightmares make us wake up with a start. An example is Pilate's wife during Jesus's trial. She said to Pilate: "Have nothing to do with that innocent man, for today I have suffered a great deal because of a dream about him" (Matt 27:19).

Good, Promising Dreams

The great dream of Pierre Teilhard de Chardin (1881–1955) was to announce a new historical era, the noosphere, a human race united in mind and heart, inhabiting the same planet. He emphasized that "The time of nations has passed; what is important is to build the Earth."

Pope Francis said jokingly to young people in Palermo in September 2018: "Better to be good dreamers than lazy realists, better to be Don Quixote than Sancho Panza," in other words, give priority to dreams rather than Sancho Panza's immobilizing calm. What is the dream of liberation theology? It is that all, beginning with the poorest and most oppressed, will be able to free themselves from the many oppressions, external and internal, and live as brothers and sisters in justice and solidarity, respectful of nature and Mother Earth, sharing one great table and enjoying, with moderation on the part of all, the good fruits of our great, generous Mother Earth. For trying to make this dream come true, many in Latin America were persecuted, imprisoned, tortured, and killed. But the dream that is true and good never dies. Hope assures us that it will come true one day.

What is Pope Francis's great dream, also shared by the Earth Charter and by so many ecologists? It is well expressed in his extraordinary encyclical *Laudato Si': On Care for Our Common Home* (June 2015), and can be summed up in this sentence: "Everything is related, and we human beings are united as brothers and sisters on a wonderful pilgrimage, woven together by the love God has for each of his creatures and which also unites us in fond affection with Brother Sun, Sister Moon, Brother River, and Mother Earth" (§92).

Either we care for Mother Earth, our Common Home, and we join hands to work together and in solidarity, or we form the procession of those headed for their own funeral. Here we see the importance and the urgency of nurturing good

dreams that lead us to transformational activities and constantly nourish our hope.

This is the dream I want to pass on, as my life moves
toward its end, to the young people who will come after us.
It is their task to take forward the dream of Jesus, of Pope
Francis, of liberation theology at its broadest, and of so many
others who also nurture dreams of a better humanity. These
young people will have to be the leaders in shaping a better
future for us, for nature, and for Mother Earth.

2

What Is This Creature That Thinks It Can Do Theology?

Before venturing to talk about God, we need to ask about human beings. Without human beings the God question loses meaning. If we lose human beings, we lose the trail that leads us to Ultimate Reality.

It is human beings who, looking at themselves, at history, at nature and the star-strewn universe, ask: who set all this going? Questions like this are unavoidable. The faith we have or don't have, or the worldview we adopt, matters little—they force themselves on the human mind.

Human Beings in the Process of Anthropogenesis

In the end, who are we, tiny sensitive creatures who think and love, on a tiny old planet, lost in the immensity of space among the stars?

When we take these questions to their most radical formulation, we all become philosophers and theologians, even if we don't use those names. But there are people who make these questions and thinking about them their life's work. They become philosophers, thinkers, and theologians of the most varied tendencies.

Taking into account all the knowledge the sciences have accumulated, we ask, perhaps with some perplexity: Who are we in the end, if we are human beings? The universe prepared all the factors and found a delicate balance of all the energies, information, and types of matter to allow for the emergence of the human being, endowed with self-consciousness and awareness of the Mystery. But to be what they are today, *sapiens*, human beings had to travel a long way. Just as there is a cosmogenesis, there is also an anthropogenesis, the emergence of human beings, men and women, through the process by which the universe, our galaxy, the Milky Way and the Earth, all evolved. Human beings are the end of a journey that began more than thirteen billion years ago.

Seventy-five million years ago, at the end of the Mesozoic period, there appeared the distant ancestors of human beings, the simians. They were small mammals, no bigger than a mouse. They lived in the tops of giant trees, trembling with fear of being devoured by the larger dinosaurs.

After the disappearance of the dinosaurs, sixty-five million years ago, these simians were able to develop unhindered. Thirty-five million years ago we find them as primates, which formed a common trunk leading to chimpanzees and other great apes on the one hand and us human beings on the other. They lived in the African forests, adapting themselves to changes in climate, as it veered from torrential rains to baking droughts.

Seven million years ago there was a decisive split as a result of a huge lowering of the Earth's surface that created the Rift Valley, which crosses a large part of Africa from north to south. On one side, in the higher area, this left the big primates, the chimpanzees and gorillas (with which we share 99 percent of our genes), in the forests, damp and rich in food resources; and on the other, the lower area, where the savannahs and dry areas appeared, were the Australopithecus, already on their way to hominization. Living in a habitat with scarce food resources, they had to develop their brain more and use only two legs, in order to see farther.

Three to four million years ago, in what are now the Afar regions of Ethiopia, Australopithecus was beginning to display humanoid characteristics. 2.6 million years ago there appeared *homo habilis*, who was now using tools (polished stones and sticks) as a way of impacting nature. 1.5 million years ago they were already walking on two legs as *homo erectus*, capable of more elaborate mental activity. But around 330 million years ago, the reptilian brain had already developed, the brain that regulates our instinctive movements such as the beating of the heart, the blinking of the eyes, and our protective reactions to an object that might injure us; and later, around 220 million years ago, the limbic brain emerged: this is present in mammals, including us, and is responsible for our inner world of feelings, concern and love, and desires and dreams.

To complete the process, seven or eight million years ago, the neocortical brain was formed; this is responsible for our rationality and mental connections. Following this sequence, around two hundred million years ago the fully human *homo sapiens* burst on to the scene, living socially, using language and organizing cooperatively in order to survive. Finally, a hundred million years ago, the modern *homo sapiens sapiens* emerged, whose brain is so complex that it makes possible conscious self-perception and intelligence.

This is what creates the biological base of the conscious perception that we are part of a greater whole and tap into that Basic Energy that fills the universe, imbuing us with respect and veneration before the Mystery that reveals and hides itself in the world, in the cosmos and in each being. We realize that a Link unites and holds together all things and with which we can enter into communion through rites, dances, songs, and speech.

Arising in Africa—which means that we are all Africans—these human beings were to begin their pilgrimage across the continents until they occupied the whole planet

and reached the present, the beginning of the great return to
the Common Home, creating the planetary phase of humanity and of the Earth itself.

From the Neolithic period, about ten million years ago,
they started to live socially in an organized way, build
towns, cities and states, cultures and civilizations, and ask
questions about the meaning of their life, their death, and
the universe, as we can see from the rock symbols and paint-
ings. They began to structure visions of the world around
that powerful and loving Energy that sustains and pervades
everything and found themselves to be open to totality and
inhabited by an infinite desire. The Mystery became more
and more sacramental, in other words, made itself known
more and more in human consciousness, which perceived in
facts not just mere facts but meanings and values.

Human beings translated their experience of the Mystery using a thousand names born of their reverence, their
ecstasy, and their love. They felt immersed in that Mystery
that gave them a meaning for their lives. They opened up
to the world around them, to other people, to the diverse
societies, to the Whole, to God. Nothing satisfied their hunger. Their cry for fulfillment is the echo of the voice of the
Mystery calling them. The Mystery may take the form of a
companion in love, a hearer of the word, a host of the Mystery perceived within oneself. A person may welcome, in the
language of Christian understanding, God-communion and
love, and that God may communicate with that person. A
human person is an infinite openness calling for the infinite. Human beings look for it tirelessly on all sides and in
all forms, but only finite objects. What infinite will come to
meet a person and fill them? An infinite void demands an
infinite object to fill it.

In the light of this view of anthropogenesis, we could say
that the human being is a manifestation of Basic Energy
from which everything derives (the Quantic Void or Original Source of all beings); a cosmic being, part of a universe

possibly, among other parallels, structured in eleven dimensions (string theory); formed by the same physical and chemical element and the same cosmic dust that make up all beings; we are inhabitants of a medium-sized galaxy, one among two hundred billion, revolving around the sun, a fifth-category star, one among three hundred billion, situated twenty-seven thousand light years from the center of the Milky Way, on the inner arm of the spiral of Orion, living on a tiny planet, the Earth, which is regarded as a super-organism that permanently regulates itself, known as Gaia, and which also gives us everything we need to live, us and the whole community of life.

We are a link in the sacred chain of life, an animal of the branch of vertebrates, sexed, belonging to the class of mammals, to the order of primates, to the family of hominids, to the genus *homo* and the species *sapiens/demens*; endowed with a body containing thirty billion cells and trillions of bacteria, constantly renewed by a genetic system formed over 3.7 billion years, the age of life. We have three brain levels, the reptilian (source of instinctive reactions), the limbic (for emotions), and the most recent, dating from seven to eight million years ago, the neocortical (responsible for language and organizing concepts).

Human beings possess a psyche with the same ancestry as the body, which allows them to be subjects. The psyche is inhabited by all sorts of emotions and structured by the principle of desire, with ancestral archetypes and crowned by the spirit, that element of consciousness by which we can perceive ourselves and feel ourselves part of a greater whole and which makes us always open to the other and to the infinite, able to impact nature, caring for it or plundering it and, in all this, able to make culture, to create and capture meanings and values and to interrogate ourselves about the ultimate meaning of everything and of the Earth, today in its planetary phase, on the way to the noosphere in which minds and hearts converge in a unified humanity. We all inhabit the Common Home, in the dream described by Pope Francis and other ecologists.

There is no one better than the mathematician and philosopher Pascal (1623–1662) to express the complex creature that we are: "What is the human being in nature? A nothing before the infinite and an everything before the nothing, a link between nothing and everything, but unable to see the nothing from which they were taken and the infinite by which they are attracted."

In the human being three infinites intersect: the infinitely small, the infinitely large, and the infinitely complex (Teilhard de Chardin and Morin). Being all this, we feel whole but incomplete and still being born, sensing ourselves full of virtual powers that are pushing to emerge but have not yet emerged. We are always in our own prehistory.

Human Beings: A Compound of *Sapiens* and *Demens*

We cannot forget a fundamental fact of the human condition. It is not a defect of creation but of its nature. Human beings are dia-bolic and sym-bolic, cruel and tender, chaos and cosmos, *sapiens* and *demens*; in other words, they are endowed with intelligence and wisdom and at the same time—I stress this—at the same time capable of excesses and acts of madness.

This complex and contradictory reality is an aspect of the structure of the universe and of every creature. We came from an immense chaos (the Big Bang), and evolution/expansion/self-creation/self-organization is a way of introducing order into this chaos. It is not just chaotic, but also capable of producing new orders, from which comes cosmos (beauty and harmony).

As everything has to do with everything else and is constantly involved in networks of relations, human beings also emerge as beings with total relationships.

If we want to describe this, without trying to define human nature, it emerges as a bundle of relationships pointing in all directions: downward, upward, inward, outward. It is like a rhizome, a bulb with roots going in all directions. Human beings construct themselves to the extent that they activate this complex of total relations.

The permanent challenge is to give direction to and keep under control the type of relationships we engage in. They can be destructive or constructive, they can have good effects and bad effects. It is here that the basic ethical project that guides our lives comes into force: since everything has to do with everything else and all creatures are interdependent, the human creature also comes into focus as a creature with total relationships.

Human beings, because they are a bundle of relationships, also have the characteristic of coming into being as an unlimited openness: to themselves, to the world, to others, and to the infinite. They feel within themselves an infinite drive that leaves them with a sense of unfulfillment; this is the source of their permanent dissatisfaction. It is not a psychological problem that can be cured by a psychoanalyst or psychiatrist; it is their distinctive feature, an ontological one and, as I said before, not a defect. This unfulfillment demands fulfillment, and this is the source of their constant hope.

In biological terms, we are needy creatures. We do not possess any organ that ensures our subsistence. We have to activate our bundle of relationships in all directions. For this reason, we are essentially social beings who construct our common habitat together with others. Civilizations were born out of this relational impulse of human beings, bundles of total relationships.

But we have a limit: life comes with death. It is hard for us to accept death as part of life, with the dramatic quality of human destiny this implies. Through love, through art, and through faith, we have a sense that death is not an end but an invention of life itself so that we can be transformed by it. And we suspect that in the final reckoning a small act of true, unconditional love is worth more than all the matter and energy of the universe combined. Because of this the only worthwhile attitude is to speak, believe in, and hope in an Ultimate Reality to which we are attracted as an extension of love in the form of the infinite.

It is part of the uniqueness of human beings that they do not just sense a living Presence, mysterious and loving, pervading all creatures, with which they can maintain a dialogue of friendship and love. They also sense that this Presence corresponds to the infinite desire they feel in themselves, an infinity that is matched with them and in which they can rest.

This Ultimate Reality is not one object among others, or some other energy among others. If that were the case, it could be detected by science, and it would not be the oceanic experience that cannot be captured by any formula. It presents itself as that support whose nature is Mystery, which sustains and nurtures everything and keeps it in existence. Without it, everything would return to nothing or to the Quantic Void from which it burst out. This Ultimate Reality is the force by which thinking thinks, but it cannot be captured by thought. It is the eye that sees everything but cannot see itself. It is the Mystery always known but always indefinitely still to be known. It pervades and penetrates the very innermost part of every human being and of the whole universe.

We can think, meditate on, and interiorize this mysterious Reality, which underlies all realities. But it is in this direction that human beings must be conceptualized. What human beings are and what their ultimate destiny is are lost in the Unknowable, always in some way knowable, which is the space of the Mystery that is known and indefinitely still to be known. So we are, as human beings, an equation that is never resolved and always remains open.

There is an additional point that we get from the new cosmology. All beings are an expression of this universe. Because their natural situation is not stability, but mutation, we talk today about cosmogenesis, instead of simply cosmology, because everything is still in genesis, in a process of being born.

We Are the Earth That Feels, Thinks, and Loves

The human being is the point at which the universe comes to itself, thinks about itself, and celebrates the grandeur of its process. As the Earth is within this cosmogenic movement, the human being arises as that portion of the Earth that at a given moment of its complexity and at the peak of its organization began to feel, think, love, and venerate. Human beings are the Earth, as the First Testament bears witness and Pope Francis's ecological encyclical *Laudato Si'* also states (§§66–68).

For this reason humans come from humus, fertile earth, and the biblical Adam is connected in Hebrew with the word for earth that can be tilled and is fertile (*adamah*). The Earth is the Pachamama revered by the indigenous peoples of the Andes, or our Great Mother. We are a part of her, that part into which spirit has exploded, and we are able to identify that mysterious, powerful, and loving Energy that pervades everything and sustains everything, the Originating Source of all beings.

The father of North American ecology, the anthropologist and theologian Thomas Berry (1914–2009) put this very well in one of his twelve principles for understanding the universe and our role within it: "The universe, the solar system, and Planet Earth in themselves and in their evolutionary emergence constitute for the human community the primary revelation of that ultimate Mystery whence all things emerge into being." This statement about the fundamental Mystery that is the origin of everything sharpens still further the question: Who are we and who will reveal our nature and destiny? No one within the confines of the world as it exists, or an ecology, however comprehensive, can really give us a satisfactory answer.

It is the task of philosophical and theological thinking to decipher this Ultimate Reality, find a name for it that we can venerate, many names—and even then we cannot define its nature as a Mystery, knowable yet still to be known. We only have signs to indicate the area in which we should think and the attitudes we should cultivate to be able to capture its mysterious and loving presence. The question about what the human being is is inseparable from the question about Ultimate Reality I mentioned earlier.

Those who profess the Christian faith simply use the name God. Others give it other names: Tao, Shiva, Olorum, and Yahweh, but it is always the same Ultimate Reality. The names change, but the Reality is always there challenging us. Both of us, the human being and God, are a mystery, each in its own way, immovable and mutually involved.

The Theologian and Wisdom

The theologian who knows only about theology ends up not even knowing theology. By its nature, theology is a globalizing discourse, because it dares to think about all things and to articulate them in the light of God. Theologians will succeed in maintaining a dialogue on a very basic level with the various branches of current knowledge only if they take this task seriously all through their lives. The reward will be a spirit of wisdom. The true theologian who tries to get at the roots must slowly become a sage. I am not saying that I have reached that stage; that would be huge arrogance (what the Greeks called *hybris*). But I have tried to open myself to it, searching for the wisdom that the

Bible talks about and praises so highly, especially the book
of Wisdom.

The wise person makes themselves sensitive to the meaning of the Mystery, to human greatness and human wretch-
edness. They make themselves able to read the world as a
symbol of a mystery that pervades all reality and also inhab-
its their own life. There is therefore a sacredness peculiar
to wisdom. The wise person's role is to discuss ends and
not just get lost in means. It is in this dimension that their
ethical and spiritual position, fundamental for any thinker,
is revealed. They are the guardian of humanity's great ide-
als; they are not concerned so much with the *how*, but principally ask about the *why*, where truth is hidden. Only the
thinker can be a martyr like Socrates and so many others in
the history of humanity, in testimony to a truth that isn't the
possession of anyone but an authority that judges everyone,
including the thinker.

The thinker does not exist just in the sphere of high culture. Since thinking is an attribute of every human being,
there are also thinkers at lower levels of society who use the
grammar of symbols and narrative to scrutinize the meaning of reality and express it with the same force and, not
infrequently, more forcefully than the typical thinker.

These days, along with people's movements, lower-class
thinkers act as the natural communications media of the
longings and struggles of the oppressed, of the questioning
of the type of society we suffer under, questions about the
sort of society we want and how to preserve the values still
not lost in popular culture.

Obviously, like any other person active in society, the
thinker also has their own place in society. In a class society like ours, with huge inequalities, the thinker also has the
organic function of denouncing this and announcing that it
can be replaced by the establishment of social justice. Nevertheless, the thinker doesn't get totally absorbed by class

definitions; their commitment is with the truth that has to be reached by thought and affirmed, whatever the difficulty, in season and out of season (2 Tim 4:2). Ignorance and cover-ups don't help anyone but harm us all.

There is an authority that does not fit into the interests of the social groups that play their roles in the great opera of life. They do not produce the truth, nor can they interpret it to suit themselves for long. Truth judges them. Supreme truth is not judged by the verdict of history; truth judges history itself. To think about truth in this way is where the thinker has to be courageous, especially when the thinker takes on the role of theologian.

As a consequence, their social position is uncomfortable because it cannot be reduced to the criteria of a social, religious, or church position. Their distinctive role is that philosophical one, so typical of the tradition of Western thought: always rethinking the very foundations, questioning their premises, recognizing the vicious circle in all thought, and making themselves able to turn it into a virtuous circle by re-examining permanently the old questions that become new as they are always considered afresh, such as the meaning of life and the Mystery of all existence. In other words, the thinker proves that, despite all the constraints of the human condition, they are never consumed by them but reach universality. As a result, there are questions that simply are human and not registered as belonging to the middle class or proletariat, the ruling class or the underclass.

The thinker's existence always makes us revisit fundamental questions: What are human beings? What are they capable of? What are they called to? Are they a growth on the cosmogenic process? Or, alternatively, do they not possess an inherent irreducibility? Are they not rather that creature through whom the very universe becomes aware of itself? What is the mysterious Light by which we see light?

What type of language does a thinker normally produce? They travel between various fields of knowledge and try to ecologize them. Their language consists, in the good sense of the word, of a semantic mix. They mix types of language, combine language games because they know that they are all interlinked in an indescribable network of relationships, as Pope Francis emphasizes so emphatically in *Laudato Si'*.

In this sense, all forms of language are at the service of the communication of what is universally human. As their role is situated at the level of fundamental questions, at one time they will philosophize like a philosopher, at another conjure up images like a poet, at another again they will reason like a scientist, or warn like a moralist, now universalize like a humanist, now adopt a priestly tone, now force language like a mystic. Their language is that of any spiritual master: they teach, admonish, summon, prophesy, maintaining a sober tone on questions relating to the Meaning of meanings, without which life loses its dignity and is no longer worth living.

Every generation has its great sages. They become great through the fidelity with which they remain listening to the Spirit in time. They are witnesses to the Spirit, like arrows pointing to the sky. Many of those who walk in the valley lift their eyes and, because of them, also try to see the mountaintops, where the High is even higher. It is an arrow pointing to those causes that give dignity to human beings and for which it is worthwhile living, sacrificing oneself, and dying with dignity.

A Theologian, an Almost Impossible Creature

After all these considerations, I have to confess humbly that doing theology is a task almost impossible to perform. It's not like watching a film or going to the theatre. It's a very serious matter because it deals with Ultimate Reality, with the Originating Principle of all being, which isn't a tangible object like everything else.

That is why looking for the "God particle" within matter, where the Higgs boson exists, makes no sense at all. That would presuppose that God was part of the world, a piece of the world, even if the most important one. I shall borrow the words of a subtle Franciscan theologian, Duns Scotus (1266–1308): "If God exists in the way things exist, then God does not exist." In other words, God is not of the order of things that can be found and described. God is the Precondition and prior Support that enables things to exist. Without God, things would have remained in that unfathomable sea of Basic Energy or would return to it.

This is the nature of God, not to be a thing, but the Origin and Generative Abyss of all things. The Origin cannot be captured by thought because it is the precondition of all thinking. As we see, doing theology is very complicated. Henri Lacordaire (1802–1861), the great French orator, said rightly: "The Catholic intellectual is an almost impossible figure: they have to know the whole deposit of faith, the acts of the papacy, and on top of that what St. Paul calls 'the elements of this world,' that is, everything and then everything."

Let us remember what René Descartes (1596–1650) asserted in his *Discourse on Method*, the basis of modern theories of knowledge: "If I wanted to do theology, I would need to be more than human." And Erasmus of Rotterdam (1466–1536), the great intellectual of the Reformation period, commented: "There is something super-human about the profession of the theologian."

It comes as no surprise that Martin Heidegger (1889–1976), perhaps the deepest philosophical thinker of recent times, should have said that a philosophy that does not address the questions of theology has not yet become a fully developed philosophy. The role of the theologian is almost impossible, something I feel every day.

Logically, there is a lazy theology that gives up thinking about God. It just thinks what others have thought or what the theologians of the past or the official documents of the popes have said. My sense of the world tells me that today theology as theology of our time has to shout as Pope Francis did in his encyclical *Laudato Si'* that we have to care for and preserve nature and get ourselves into harmony with the universe, because these constitute the first great book God gave us. It is there that we find what God wants to say to us. Because we forgot how to read this book, in his mercy God gave us another one, the Judeo-Christian Scriptures and those of other peoples, so that we could relearn to read the book of nature and of the universe. Today the Common Home is being devastated, and by devastating it we are destroying our access to God's revelation. This means we have to talk about nature and the world both in the light of God and of scientific reasoning. If nature and the world are not preserved, the sacred books would lose their point, which is to teach us once more to read the book of nature and the world.

The language of theology, after all, takes its place alongside all the other languages, which, when taken to their utmost radical form, also address the Mystery of all things. It was this Mystery character that fascinated Einstein (1879–1955). A person who doesn't realize this, he said, is like a blind person who has no sight at all.

We dare to give this Mystery a name, a name of reverence and adoration: the God of a thousand names and infinite attributes. The dignity of the human being resides in this capacity to ask questions and to enter into dialogue with this Mystery that, in the end, can be felt in the human heart.

3

God, the Originating Principle of All Beings

Now we come to that Ultimate Reality that we customarily call God. This is the greatest challenge to radical thinking and theology.

Long ago the medieval thinkers St. Thomas Aquinas (1225–1274), St. Bonaventure (1221–1274), and Duns Scotus (1266–1308), among others, taught that theology as such is the knowledge God has of God, in other words, God's divine thinking, idea, and mystery. That is inaccessible to us. It is God for God.

But in human terms, theology is reflection on God and on all things in the light of God. In other words, nothing escapes the divine sphere. For example, we can always ask: What is politics like in the light of God, or how does God reveal or withhold himself in politics? What is science and technology from God's perspective? Does it serve life or corporate enrichment? How does God enter, internally and externally, into the historical and social liberation of the oppressed? In other words, we can do theology about anything, provided that we keep God's perspective.

This is the sense in which the churches intervene in politics, economics, on social issues, and in other fields, always starting from the theological perspective and the ethics that that view inspires. They don't talk politically about politics, but talk about it in a theological way, or in gospel terms, because that is their specific field. Outside that field they lose legitimacy.

God as Intrinsic Mystery and for Us

Thousands of names have been given to the entity "God." All are insufficient because the adequate words cannot be found in any dictionary of any language. For that reason, as I have mentioned already, the word "mystery" would be the most adequate.

But be careful: Mystery is not the same as a problem that disappears as soon as it is solved. Mystery is what we can come to know, but is not exhausted by any knowledge. It remains a mystery even when it is known. Albert Einstein put it well: "A person who does not have their eyes open to Mystery will go through life not seeing anything." This is the most appropriate understanding of the Mystery of God. For this reason, the Mystery is always dynamic. We only know it partially. As it is always dynamic, we may dare to say that God is a mystery even for God. That is God's true nature, as some mystics have already asserted. But there is one difference between us and God: God's knowledge of God's Mystery is constantly full and complete, whereas ours is always limited and partial.

Because it is dynamic, the divine Mystery is always open to a new fullness, remaining always an eternal and infinite Mystery for itself. In this sense Mystery-God has a future. God can be what God has never previously been, as with God's incarnation in the man Jesus of Nazareth. We are making an assumption about what those who know God from experience, the mystics, testify. They often say that when we talk about God we are making more denials than assertions; we speak more falsehoods than truths. Despite this, we must speak about God with reverence and holy fear, because we are raising questions that can only be given feeble responses by appealing to the category "God," as I said in the last chapter.

The word "God" embodies the unlimited extent of our imaging and the highest utopia of order, harmony, consciousness, passion, and supreme meaning that moves people and cultures. The word "God" possesses existential significance only if it takes human sentiments to these dimensions, in the mode of infinity and supreme plenitude.

There are many ways to talk about God, as the history of religions, theology, and the mystics bears witness. I want to take a path for our time, one that is relatively new, and comes from the new cosmology (the science of the cosmos), since in it the scientists themselves encounter the Mystery and say so explicitly. In the first place, what fascinates scientists is the harmony and beauty of the universe. Everything seems to have been set up so that, from the bottomless depths of an ocean of primordial energy, there necessarily would emerge the elementary particles, then organized matter, subsequently complex matter, which is life, and finally matter in a complete harmony of vibrations, forming a supreme holistic unity, consciousness. In the terms of those who formulated the strong and weak anthropic principle (to what extent human beings are part of the interpretation of the universe), Brandon Carter, Hubert Reeves, and others, if things had not occurred as they did (the expansion/explosion, the formation of the big red stars, the galaxies, the stars, the planets, etc.), we would not be here to say all that we are saying.

In other words, for us to be here, all the cosmic factors in all the 13.7 billion years of existence of our known universe had to be articulated and converge in such a way as to make possible complexity, life, and consciousness. Had this not happened, we would not exist and be here to think about such things.

Accordingly, everything is involved with everything else: when I lift a pen from the ground I come into contact with the gravitational force that attracts all the bodies of the universe or allows them to fall. If, for example, the density of the universe in the ten seconds after the expansion/explosion had not maintained its adequate critical level, the universe could never have formed; matter and antimatter would have cancelled each other out, and there would not have been sufficient cohesion for the formation of masses and so of matter.

We find a meticulous calibration of measurements without which the stars would never have come into being or life exploded in the universe. For example, if strong nuclear interaction (what maintains the cohesion of the nuclei of atoms) had been 1 percent more powerful, hydrogen would never have been formed to combine with oxygen and give us water, which is essential to living creatures. If electromagnetic energy (which gives cohesion to atoms and molecules and allows chemical combinations) had increased just a little, there would have been no chance of the formation of the DNA chain and so of the production and reproduction of life. This was summed up very well by the British American physicist Freeman Dyson (1923–2020): "The more I examine the universe and study the details of its architecture, the more evidence I find that the universe in some sense must have known that we were coming" (*Disturbing the Universe* [New York: Basic Books, 1979], 250).

In each thing we find everything, forces interacting, particles relating to each other, matter stabilizing, openness for new relationships coming into being, and life creating ever more complex orders. All things display the trademark of the divine and of nature, a signature that transmits messages that we have to decipher. Finding that this order existed in the universe produced in scientists such as Einstein, Bohm, Hawking, Prigogine, Swimme, and others feelings of amazement and veneration. This order is pervaded by a consciousness and spirit from its first moment. This implicit order points to an underlying Supreme Order, as David Bohm, Einstein's favorite pupil, emphasized. Consciousness and spirit point to a Consciousness beyond this cosmos and a transcendent Spirit.

How God Emerges in the Cosmogenic Process

How are we to explain the existence of being? What was there before the inflationary universe and before the Big Bang? There is Max Planck's Wall, the ultimate limit that prevents us from seeing the other side of things. About this science has nothing to say; it starts from the universe as already formed. But the scientist, as a human being, does not stop asking such questions. Max Planck, the formulator of quantum theory, rightly wrote: "Science cannot solve the ultimate Mystery of nature because in the last analysis we ourselves are part of nature and so of the Mystery we seek to uncover."

The silence of science does not smother all words. There is still a last word that comes from the other field of human knowledge, from theology, from spirituality, and from the religions. For this, knowing is not to stand at a distance from reality to expose it in its parts. Knowing is a form of love, participation, and communion; it is the discovery of the whole beyond the parts, of the synthesis beyond the analysis. Coming to know means discovering oneself within the totality, internalizing it and diving into it.

The truth is that we only know well what we love. The physicist David Bohm, who was also a mystic, insisted: "We might imagine a mystic as someone who is in contact with the frightening depths of matter or of the subtle mind, whatever name we give to it." We have called it God. From astonishment came science as the effort to decipher the hidden code of all phenomena. From veneration come mysticism, theology, and the ethics of care and universal responsibility. Science wants to explain how things exist, as Ludwig Wittgenstein (1889–1951) argued in his *Tractatus Logico-*

Philosophicus. Mysticism is ecstatic at the fact that things are and exist; it venerates the One who reveals themselves and veils themselves behind each thing and everything; it tries to experience it and establish communions with It. What mathematics is for the scientist is meditation for the mystic and the theologian's reverent reflection. The physicist seeks matter down to its last possible division, down to the ultimate ability to detect it, and arrives at the areas of energy and the quantic vacuum (the Originating Principle of all being). Mysticism and theology, carried out with reverence, capture the Energy that condenses at many levels until it reveals itself as the Mystery of God or the God of the Mystery.

Today more and more scientists, sages, theologians, and mystics find themselves astonished and in veneration before the Mystery of the universe. They know that both derive from the same basic experience, that both point in the same direction, toward the Mystery of reality, known rationally by science and experienced emotionally by spirituality, mysticism, and theology. Everything converges toward the One who is Nameless, provisionally labeled by cosmologists as "Basic Energy," the "Abyss that Nurtures Everything," or the "Original Source of all beings."

What outline can we trace of the image of God that bursts from the cosmological reflection of our time? It derives from the "chain of references" research is forced to carry out: from matter we are referred back to the atom, to elementary particles, from these to Basic Energy, also called the Quantic Vacuum, which is nothing like a vacuum because it is the repository of all the virtualities and potentialities of the universe. This Energy is the last reference point of analytical reason. Everything comes from it and everything returns to it. It is the boundless ocean of energies, the continent of all possibilities, of everything that can happen. It may also be the "great attractor" of the cosmos, because we find that the whole universe is being attracted by a mysterious central point.

But Basic Energy still belongs to the order of the universe, although it has the characteristics we attribute to God: it cannot be named, is infinite, generates everything. What happened before time? What existed before the before? It is the atemporal reality in the absolute equilibrium of its movement, the totality of perfect symmetry, Energy without end and Force without boundaries. It is God in God's Mystery.

At a "moment" in the divine plenitude, God decided to create a mirror in which he could see himself. God created companions for his life and his love. To create is to decay, that is, to allow something to appear that is not God and does not have God's exclusive characteristics (plenitude, absolute symmetry, life without entropy, coexistence of all opposites). Something of that original plenitude decays. So decadence here has an ontological sense (it is part of the structure of reality) rather than an ethical one.

God created that dot, billions of times smaller than a pinhead, and an immeasurable flow of energy is transferred into it. There all probabilities and possibilities are on display. A universal wave is in action. The Supreme Observer (God) observes them and enables some to materialize, to combine with others. The others collapse and return to the realm of probabilities, to Basic Energy.

Everything expands and then explodes. There is suddenly a universe in expansion. The Big Bang, rather than a starting point, is a point of instability that makes possible, through the relationships of everything with everything else, the emergence of holistic units and increasingly interrelated orders. The universe in formation is nothing less than the image of God, an image of God's potency in being and being alive.

If everything in the universe makes up a web of relationships, if everything is in communion with everything, as Pope Francis keeps emphasizing in his encyclical *Laudato Si'*, if the image of God is presented shaped in the form of communion, it is a sign that this supreme Reality is also fundamentally and essentially communion, life in relatedness and supreme love: "For Christians, believing in one God who is trinitarian communion suggests that the Trinity has left its mark on all creation. . . . The Divine Persons are subsistent relations, and the world, created according to the divine model, is a web of relationships" (*Laudato Si'*, §§239–40).

This reflection is in accordance with the testimony of humanity's mystical intuitions and spiritual traditions. The essence of Judeo-Christian experience runs along this line, that of a God in communion with God's creation, of a personal God, a life that, according to the Christian faith, is displayed in three Living Ones, the Father, the Son, and the Holy Spirit.

The dynamic principle of self-organization that governs the universe is acting in every one of the parts and of the whole, without a name and without an image. As I said earlier, God is the name religions have found to take God from anonymity and insert God into our awareness and our celebration.

It is a name of Mystery, and expression of our reverence. It is at the heart of the universe. Human beings feel it in their hearts as a form of enthusiasm (the Greek word for "enthusiasm" means having a god within oneself). We feel integrated into it as children. Christian experience bears witness that it has come close to us, become poor among the poor so that no one should feel excluded.

It is the deepest sense of the incarnation of the Son of the Father, who came to us to take us to the dwelling the Father has prepared for us from all eternity. The fundamental human yearning is not just to know about God by hearsay (1 John 1:1), but to experience God. In our time it is the ecological attitude, especially a deep and comprehensive ecology, that best makes space for such an experience of God. We then plunge into that Mystery that surrounds everything, penetrates everything, shines through everything, supports everything, and embraces everything.

But to gain access to God there is not just one path and one door. That is the Western illusion, especially that of the Christian churches, with their claim to a monopoly on divine revelation and the means of salvation. God has always given himself and gives himself to all, in all times and places, because all of us are God's beloved sons and daughters: "Long ago God spoke . . . in many and various ways" (Heb 1:1).

For anyone who has once experienced the Mystery we call God, everything is a path, and every creature becomes a sacrament and door for meeting God. Life, despite its tribulations and the difficult combinations of chaos and cosmos and diabolical and symbolic dimensions I mentioned in the previous chapter, can turn into a feast and celebration for all eternity.

God as Trinity, Communion of Divine Persons: Christianity

Many religions argue for monotheism, the existence of one God, the Creator and Sustainer of all beings. Judaism and Islam, for example, strongly insist on the existence of one God. The Christian faith does not deny this assertion but says that it is a pre-trinitarian monotheism. It asserts the Trinity of God—Father, Son, and Holy Spirit—who give rise, through the eternally existing relationships between them, to a God who is communion, love, and communication.

Christianity comes to this affirmation because of Jesus of Nazareth, who called God his sweet Abba, which means "my Dear Daddy." Whoever calls God Father feels to be God's child. Jesus went so far as to say, "The Father and I are one" (John 10:30), or "Whoever has seen me has seen my Father" (John 14:9). And then there was a divine force active in him that made him cure sick people, free people with psychological problems (at the time they were said to be possessed by demons), and even raise the dead. He was the bearer of this divine force, which was identified as the Holy Spirit. They make up the Most Holy Trinity, Father, Son, and Holy Spirit.

They are intertwined, they interpenetrate each other, and are unified (become one) without ceasing to be different and a single Mystery. They are different so that they can relate to each other, by virtue of the other, with the other, and in the other, without ever being the other. And in this way they remain eternally together. In the beginning there is not the loneliness of the One (monotheism) but the communion of the Three (Trinity). The Three is not a number that can always be multiplied or can have another number added to it, as the philosopher Immanuel Kant (1724–1804) thought. He did not understand that the Divine Persons are unique, that unique beings are not numbers and therefore cannot be added or multiplied. But they are relational. Accordingly, they relate to each other so radically and intertwine with each other so completely that they emerge as one God who is relation, communion, and love. They are one and the same Mystery coming to being eternally in the person of the Father, in the person of the Son, and in the person of the Holy Spirit. This Mystery expresses the union of the Father and the Son of the Father and of the Holy Spirit, which is the bond of union between them.

Here we have trinitarian monotheism, a peculiarity of the Christian faith. It has always existed, it always exists, and will always exist forever. Theological understanding surrenders in reverence to the Mystery because it is aware that God the Trinity may be something our intelligence can barely grasp. If God the Trinity is essentially relationship, everything that God created will also be a relationship of everything with everything else. It is the reflection of this unnameable but loving Mystery.

A *Theologoumenon*: The Whole
Trinity Comes to Us

By *theologoumenon* we mean a theological hypothesis that is not yet an official doctrine but has a serious theological underpinning. We use a saying very widespread among medieval theologians, especially in the Franciscan tradition: *Deus potuit, decuit, ergo fecit*: "God could, it was appropriate, and so God did." Since no one can put limits on God and God is a being of absolute self-communication—inward between the three Divine Persons and outward to the universe and to human beings—this maxim makes sense: "God could, it was appropriate, and so God did it." This *theologoumenon* hypothetically supports the view that not only the Son of the Father came to us and became incarnate in our contradictory and complex humanity but also the Holy Spirit.

It is part of the essence of the Christian faith to affirm the incarnation of the Son of the Father in the human figure of Jesus. About this there is no room for argument, and we can take it as accepted by all Christians. But for there to be incarnation there had to be a woman (Miriam of Nazareth) to receive in her womb as her offspring the Son of the Father.

Something took place here to which theology has paid practically no attention. Saint Luke says explicitly that the "Holy Spirit came upon her and pitched his tent in her" (Luke 1:35). The same Greek verb is used here (*episkiasei*, which comes from *skēnē*, "tent," permanent home) as St. John uses in the prologue of his Gospel to describe the incarnation of the Word (*eskēnōsen*, which also comes from *skēnē*). In other words, the Spirit came, but did not go away, and established his permanent dwelling in Mary. When she gave her fiat (Luke 1:38), she was raised to the height of the divine. Accordingly we are told: "the holy one to be born of you will be called the Son of God" (Luke 1:35).

From this it can be deduced that the first Divine Person sent into the world was not the Son of the Father but the

Holy Spirit, who came to rest in Mary. Without her consent (fiat) the incarnation would not have happened.

That the Spirit should have come to reside in a woman is appropriate because in all Middle Eastern languages, including Hebrew, "spirit" is feminine. Thus, there is a perfect equivalence between the woman Mary and the Holy Spirit. Just as in the case of the Son we talk of incarnation, here too we can create an appropriate word, a spiritualization of Mary; in other words, Mary is inhabited by the Holy Spirit and so is spiritualized. With this spiritualization, the feminine (*anima*), which is explicitly in women and implicitly in us men (*animus*), gains its highest exaltation.

At one moment in history everything is centered on this insignificant poor woman, Miriam of Nazareth; within her grows the holy humanity of the Son of the Father; in her are present the two Divine Persons, the Holy Spirit and the Son of the Father. It is not without reason that in many representations—for example, the greatest of them, the Virgin Mother of Guadalupe, in Mexico, she is shown as pregnant and is rightly adored by the faithful who flock there in the millions. They adore the Son of the Father and the Holy Spirit who is accomplishing his incarnation among us. God could do it, it was appropriate, and so he did it: the elevation of Miriam of Nazareth to the height of divinity.

And what about the Father? We know that the three Divine Persons, because of the bond of eternal communion between them, always act together, each in his own way. The Father was not left out; he sent the Holy Spirit and his Son into humanity—phrased in cosmogenic terms, into the process of the universe in evolution. The universe will forever be marked by the presence of these Divine Persons.

It is in the Father that the Mystery shows itself as a radical Mystery. The Father is unutterable, but he is always the Father of the Son in the power of the Holy Spirit. The Father does not speak. The one who speaks is the Son, the eternal

Word, simply the Word. The Father works in silence (John 5:17), and creation is attributed to him. The Spirit's role is to give it order (Gen 1–2).

Joseph, the worker, Mediterranean craftsman and countryman, never spoke, but only had dreams (Matt 1:16, 20). We have already thought about how psychologically a dream is the way the deepest Mystery is revealed. There is therefore an equivalence between Joseph of Nazareth, the worker, and the Mystery Father, the creator. It was appropriate that the Father should find someone adequate to his nature of source Mystery, Joseph of Nazareth. He *was able to do it, it was appropriate, and so he made his entry* into our history (*potuit, decuit, ergo fecit*).

Now the Father united with his Son and the Holy Spirit and came to live and sanctify humanity and the whole universe. The Father acquires a personality in the historical figure of the anonymous widower, husband of Miriam of Nazareth, the craftsman and countryman Joseph. He possesses mystery characteristics like the Father: no one knows who was his father—the evangelist Matthew says it was Jacob (Matt 1:16)—or where he was born or where he died. He remains a mystery, suitable to personify the Mystery of the Father. Just as we spoke of the spiritualization of the Spirit in Mary and the incarnation of the Son in Jesus of Nazareth, we can talk of the paternalization of the Father in Joseph. Now the God of the Christian faith, the Trinity (the Father, the Son, and the Holy Spirit) lives definitively among us and has entered into the cosmogenic process, aligning it with its supreme realization when, as Teilhard de Chardin put it, it all implodes and explodes into the trinitarian Mystery.

In an obscure place in Palestine, Nazareth—so insignificant that it is never mentioned elsewhere in the Scriptures—outside the centers where history is made, news is passed on, and chroniclers comment—there took place the greatest event in history, the total coming, without reservation, of God the Trinity into our midst. Now we can be at peace. God the Trinity is always on our side, within the processes of history and the great universal process of cosmogenesis and anthropogenesis. Only by the light of faith can we assert such realities, but, as theologians, we may not keep silent but must announce as good news this indescribable and blessed presence of God who is relationship, communion, and love in our earthly pilgrimage.

4

The Son of the Father Is among Us: Jesus of Nazareth

Let us keep silence and contemplate: the Son of the Father is among us in the figure of the man Jesus of Nazareth, who was born in a manger "because there was no place for them in the inn" (Luke 2:7). Who can say that they have a God so close? He is a man among men. He learns the trade of his father, Joseph, a manual worker, a jack-of-all-trades, who fixes roofs, puts up walls, makes household utensils, and at the same time works as a farmer to keep his family fed.

The Incarnation of the Son of the Father

But in him dwells the eternal Son, the one who is the Word through which the Mystery abandons its hidden character and makes itself known. The Son does not become incarnate in a king, or in a high priest, or in a wise man, one who knows the Scriptures and the things of the world.

He makes his own our flesh, in other words, our human condition, complex and vulnerable, "subject to weakness" (Heb 5:2). He is familiar with joy and sadness, anger and compassion, and "learned obedience through what he suffered" (Heb 5:8). He is the same as us in everything. The physical and chemical elements and the cosmic dust that are part of us also make up his holy humanity.

But in this humanity there is a difference: as a man, he is entirely and totally open to receiving the Son of the Father. In the childish terms of affection he calls him "Dear Daddy." "Dear Daddy" can only be said by someone who really feels themselves to be a Son in the absolute sense. The incarnation is taking place. Now and forever and ever, he will be among us participating in our happy and tragic destiny.

Surely it is the first time that in our galaxy, in our solar system, and on our Earth someone has the sense of being son of Abba God and comes to live definitively among us.

In his life, word, and work he reveals the hidden Mystery, now revealed in human form. As a Son, he feels that the Father is working, and he is working with him (John 5:17).

In feeling himself the Son of Abba God, he has created the possibility that every human being, man and woman, may also feel themselves a son or daughter of God, since we all bear the same human nature. If that nature is adopted by the Son, all the members of that nature are part of the Son and become, by participation, also sons and daughters of God in the Son. It is the apex of the awareness and understanding of the dignity of the human being.

I do not want to minimize the historic act of the Nazarene (a word that at the time had a pejorative sense of a poor nobody) but simply mention that he became a wandering prophet, a great teller of stories full of wisdom, and that he had a secret power over the negative dimension of life. As a result, he had a deep compassion for those who suffered; he cured them and performed real miracles. Breaking with the prejudices of the time, he made friends with women, loved the sisters Martha and Mary, and treated with affection Mary Magdalene, the adulteress, and the Samaritan woman, and others who were close followers.

In a phrase used by Peter to the military officer, the commander of the Italian Cohort in Caesarea, "He went about doing good and healing all who were oppressed" (Acts 10:38; cf. Luke 4:18; John 3:2).

Jesuology versus Christology

Now, to understand better the meaning of the incarnation of the Son of God, we need to make a distinction, though not a separation, between Jesuology and Christology.

Jesuology: The Historical Jesus

Jesuology puts the main emphasis on the man Jesus of Nazareth, his words and actions, and so the historical Jesus occupies the center. We must never empty Jesus of his humanity on the pretext of recognizing his divinity as Son of God, or vice versa.

Jesus did not begin by proclaiming himself or the church. He proclaimed his great dream, the Kingdom of God, as we shall see later. It was a dangerous political act to proclaim the Kingdom of God as opposed to the kingdom of the Caesars. It was a challenge and a crime of *lèse-majesté*.

But he did proclaim it, saying that it was already in our midst. Because of this the authorities of the time, both religious and political, placed him under surveillance. Above all, they started a process of defamation, calling him mad (Mark 3:21), a drinker and a glutton (Matt 11:19), a blasphemer (Mark 2:7), possessed by demons, and even a subversive (Luke 23:2). They plotted his death (Mark 3:6) and finally condemned him to crucifixion (John 11:47–53).

He was a libertarian in relation to the laws and traditions that weighed down human life. Closer to God than the priests, freer than the legal experts, more ethical than the moralists, and more transformative than the revolutionaries, Jesus showed us that the supreme values of the Father are unconditional love and mercy, and that the first heirs to the Kingdom are the poor, the persecuted, and those who thirst for justice. He called them blessed. They were at the center of his liberating activity.

The Nicaraguan Christians got their theology right when they sang in their *Misa Campesina*:

A thousand times I praise you
because you were rebellious
and struggled night and day
against humanity's injustices.

Despite the slander, he continued his path and his proclamation undaunted. But he took precautions to avoid death. After the Sanhedrin's decision to kill him (John 11:47–53), he went to the town of Ephraim, near the desert, a city of refuge for those who were persecuted (John 11:54).

On the Mount of Olives he showed his complete humanity: he went into a panic to the point of sweating blood. He prayed: "Abba, Father, for you all things are possible; remove this cup from me; yet, not what I want, but what you want" (Mark 14:36).

He was arrested, put through a double trial, one religious and another political, tortured—according to some interpreters he suffered sexual violence—and crucified, a punishment inflicted on rebels.

His cry, the most mysterious of all—perhaps this was Jesus's great temptation—is preserved in Hebrew, which testifies to its authenticity. Jesus "cried out with a loud voice *Eloi, Eloi, lema sabachthani?*" which means, "My God, my God, why have you forsaken me?" "Then Jesus gave a loud cry and breathed his last" (Mark 15:36).

It was the temptation of hope. But we know from other sources that this was not his last word. The expression of overcoming his radical existential crisis was "Father, into your hands I commend my spirit" (Luke 23:46). The resurrection confirmed the truth of Jesus's dream.

Producing this summary account of the historical Jesus is the task of Jesuology. It has as the first consequence living as Jesus lived, with courage, alongside the poor and oppressed, and always faithful to the Father. He came to teach us to live the good things of the Kingdom, which are mainly unconditional love (for enemies as well), compassion for those who suffer, mercy for sinners and the bad, and loving openness to the Abba God whose goodness is infinite.

Jesuology can be summed up as following Jesus, as Pope Francis has always insisted, and is the central plank of the spirituality of liberation.

Christology: The Christ of Faith

Christology, as the name makes clear, puts the Christ of faith at the center, without disregarding the historical Jesus. Everything began with the admiration of the people for the liberation he was bringing. They began to describe him in fairly modest titles: Master, Prophet, Good, Just, and Holy. But because none of these were sufficient, they started to call him Son of David, Son of Man, Messiah-Christ, Lord, Savior of the World.

In fifty years, all the honorific titles of Roman and Greek culture were attributed to Jesus. By the end of the first century, with the evangelist John, his followers ended up calling him God. Basically, they were forced into this reasoning: a human being like Jesus could only be God himself, the Son of God.

This is the base of Christology, starting from the more divine dimension of Jesus, present in the descriptions applied to him. These gradually intensified over the centuries, such as Pantocrator (universal Lord), Christ the King, and Teilhard de Chardin's Cosmic Christ and Omega Point.

There is a danger that all these titles end up obscuring the ordinary man, our brother, who traveled among us along the dusty and stony roads of Palestine and identified himself particularly with the poor and suffering of this world.

We have to learn to make the two tendencies work together, Jesuology, which preserves the specific historical character of Jesus, and Christology, which discovers in this particular man the presence of the Son of God, the Christ-Messiah expected by the people. One tendency stresses what the First Letter of St. John puts very well: "What we have heard, what we have seen with our eyes, what we have looked at and touched with our hands" (1 John 1), in other words, a human being among other human beings. The other tendency unveils the mystery hiding behind that humanity, the living and burning presence of the Son of God among us.

However, the most convincing approach for people of today, who have difficulties with belief in God, is to present the human figure of Jesus. No one is against him: his goodness and his humanitarian ideas are on such a scale that many people, of all religious traditions, respect him and, what is more, accept him. He is a teacher for all humanity who makes us more human, more caring, more compassionate, and more open to universal forgiveness and reconciliation, and also more sensitive to the presence of the Generative Principle of all beings in nature and the universe, in other words, God.

For us Christians, we start to follow the historical Jesus and come to the Christ of faith. He is the same Divine Person, the Son of God incarnate, who is inserted into the cosmogenic process like the rest of us and accompanies us as his brothers and sisters. Accordingly, we not only venerate him, but also adore him as the Son of God, with the same nature as all three Divine Persons.

Jesus's Great Dream: The Kingdom of God

We have now reached the central point of our reflection on the Son of God who entered definitively into our history. What was he ultimately about? What was his fundamental aim?

We can reply in harmony with all the Gospels: Jesus's great dream was to proclaim, prepare, anticipate, and bring about, in the framework of our history, the *Kingdom of God*.

The phrase "Kingdom of God" occurs 122 times in the Gospels and 90 times on the lips of Jesus. It is not a territory, but a new order of things, following the plans of Trinity God; nor is it merely spiritual, but includes all aspects of reality. This is related to the absolute revolution and total liberation of all that belongs to our life and nature. It is the most radical dream ever offered to humanity, a dream anticipated in the many dreams human beings have nurtured.

Jesus is emphatic and asserts: "The time of waiting has ended. The Kingdom of God is coming. Change your lives and believe in this good news" (Mark 1:15). The signs of the presence of the Kingdom are that the lame walk, the blind see, and the dead are raised to life. Jesus explicitly announces his program in the synagogue at Nazareth: "The Spirit of the Lord is upon me, because he has anointed me to bring good news to the poor. He has sent me to proclaim release to the captives and recovery of sight to the blind, to let the oppressed go free" (Luke 4:18). As we see, it is a real liberation, liberation from what afflicts the human condition.

But this Kingdom is continually confronted with the anti-Kingdom, expressed in hate, pharisaism, legalism, discrimination against those suffering from any kind of disease, hardness of heart, and rejection of God's call. Kingdom and anti-Kingdom are in opposition.

Jesus was condemned and raised high on the cross not because this was simply the Father's will. If that were so, the Son's Father would be cruel. What the Father wanted of the Son was faithfulness taken to the extreme of giving up his own life. And that is what he did, with great suffering. As St. John says with infinite sadness, "He came to what was his own, and his own people did not accept him" (John 1:11).

Did the Kingdom fail? The answer was Jesus's resurrection. As Origen of Alexandria (184–253), one of the most brilliant Christian intellectuals, put it well, "The resurrection is the achievement of the Kingdom of God in the man Jesus." It is an anticipation of its future establishment.

Saint Paul, meditating on the risen Jesus, sees him as the

last Adam (1 Cor 15:45), the new human being. This is not the reanimation of a corpse, as in the case of Lazarus, who subsequently died, but the bursting in of a new type of human being, totally transfigured. It is as though all the possibilities and potentialities present in the human being had been realized. He really is the *new Adam*.

The Risen One as the Cosmic Christ

Being risen, Christ is beyond space and time. He has taken on a cosmic dimension, as described in the prologue of John's Gospel and in St. Paul's Epistles to the Ephesians and Colossians. The Pauline Epistles call him the *pleroma*, a Greek expression meaning fullness in everything, so that "all things have been created through him and for him. He himself is before all things, and in him all things hold together" (Col 1:16–17). Almost exaggerating, Paul insists: "He is all in all" (*panta en pasin ho Christos*, Col 3:11).

This cosmic Christology was first formulated in the work of the most subtle of Franciscan theologians, Duns Scotus. This, as well as biblical texts, provided the basis for the great cosmic Christology of Pierre Teilhard de Chardin. His achievement, as a scientist and theologian, was to insert the risen Christ into the process of evolution: Christ draws it to its culmination in an Omega Point, in which the whole of creation implodes and explodes into the Mystery of the Trinity.

Paragraph 77 of the Coptic *Gospel of Thomas*, written around AD 50—before the canonical Gospels—has had great attention from theologians, because in it the cosmic dimension of the Risen One is clear. In saying 70 Jesus says: "I am the light that is above all things: the universe went out from me and the universe returns to me. Crack the firewood and I am within it. Lift the stone and I am underneath it. For I shall be with you all days, until the end of time."

Here there is an assertion in graphic detail of the *pleroma* of the Risen One. He is in the firewood and in the stone. There are no limits to his new reality, which will also be ours.

Nothing better emphasizes the relationship of the Risen One with the cosmos than Teilhard's prayer when, one Easter Sunday, he was in the Gobi Desert in China: "Since today, Lord, I, your priest, have neither bread nor wine, nor an altar, I shall stretch my hands out over the whole universe and take all its immensity as the material of my sacrifice. Is the infinite cycle of things not the host you wish to transform? Is not the boiling crucible in which all the activities of the whole living cosmic substance are mixed and boil the chalice of suffering you wish to transform? May it be repeated today and tomorrow and forever, as long as that divine utterance *Hoc est corpus meum* ('This is my body') is not entirely fulfilled."

What Jesus Really Wanted: The Our Father and Our Bread

After developing some theological reflections, we have to ask: in the end, what was Jesus's original intention? Apart from proclaiming the Kingdom, we can answer: it was the Our Father.

We say that the Our Father and his words about "our bread" are the very words of Jesus, that is, Jesus's own voice. Why do we dare to claim this?

Because in the Our Father we do not find anything of what is important to the later church: Jesus himself as savior, his death and resurrection, the church, the creed, the sacraments, and the dogmas. There's no mention of any of these. For Jesus these are not the most important things. What is important, what is essential is our Abba God and his Kingdom, and our daily Bread, which meets the needs of human beings.

This is the absolute minimum of Jesus's message. If someone asks, "In the end, what did Jesus want?," we have to reply:

he wanted to bring the Kingdom of God, wanted us to think of God as a loving Daddy (Abba), with characteristics of a mother, thus our Father. And he wanted us to look for our bread. Notice: he doesn't say "my Father" but "our Father." He doesn't say "my bread" but "our bread." With this phrasing, Jesus goes beyond any private devotion or individualism and places the community at the center. This is Jesus's core intention, Jesus's original intention. Everything else is commentary.

In this way the Our Father matches a human being's three fundamental and inevitable hungers:

1. The first hunger is for a meeting with Someone good, who wraps me in their arms, which means welcome and joy in life. This hunger for Someone is our *kind Daddy* (Abba).
2. The second hunger is the infinite hunger that is never satisfied, the dream of a full meaning for life, for history, and for the universe. This comes with the name Kingdom of God, the dream dreamed and preached by Jesus, the dream of an absolute revolution and a good end for all things.
3. There is yet another hunger, a hunger that is satisfied, but without which we cannot live; this is our daily bread. Without this material basis, talking about our Father and the Kingdom loses its meaning, because a corpse has no religion, doesn't call on the Father or wait for the Kingdom.

As we see, Jesus formulates his message based on a human being's deepest quests and yearnings. He gives them an answer that anyone can understand, one that is extremely humanitarian.

If we look carefully, we see that the prayer brings together a human being's two radical drives, the drive upward, toward the universe and toward that Originating Source that created everything, toward our Father. At the same time it engages the drive downward, toward the earth and toward bread, without which no one can live.

The cause of the Father—the Kingdom—and the human cause—bread—converge. They only meet in the legacy of Jesus, who keeps permanently united our bread and our Father. That is why we can say Amen.

The first Christians knew that this prayer concealed the most original message of Jesus. It belonged to what was called the *disciplina arcani*, that is, it was taught only to those who had already been initiated into the Christian faith and baptized. Tertullian (160–220), the greatest lay theologian of early Christianity, says it with emphasis: the Our Father is the *breviarium totius Evangelii*, the summary of the whole gospel.

Apart from the Our Father, there are also indications of Jesus's original intention in his forty-one parables, even though they have been reworked theologically and in literary form by the authors of the four Gospels. But the core is from Jesus.

They are taken from accounts of everyday life at that time, full of life and color. Their point is to explain the nature of the Kingdom that is already present, in process, and still in the future. Some are unforgettable, such as that of the Prodigal Son (Luke 15:11–32), the Good Samaritan (Luke 10:25–37), the Rich Man and Lazarus (Luke 16:1–7), the arrogant Pharisee and the humble tax collector (Luke 18:9–14), the Weeds among the Wheat (Matt 13:24–30, 36–43), the Great Dinner (Luke 14:16–24), and the scene of the Last Judgment (Matt 25:31–46).

In conclusion, we can say: with Jesus there was inaugurated a faster process of the coming and establishment of the Kingdom as a total revolution and liberation of the universe, of humanity, and of people's lives.

He was concerned with the celestial and transcendent

dimension of human beings, pointed upward, toward our Father, and waiting for the Kingdom. And he was also concerned with the earthly and immanent dimension, pointed toward the earth and the daily bread that is everyone's and for everyone.

Combining these two dimensions under the rainbow of the Kingdom of God depends on the support of people who constantly increase the space in which the Kingdom is established in the union of our Father in heaven and our bread on earth, in solidarity, love, forgiveness, compassion, in thirst for justice, in faithfulness to the truth, in total confidence and surrender to Abba God, and in acceptance of his Son.

This Kingdom lives with the risk of being frustrated, denied, and finally rejected. Dramatically, that is what happened in the life of Jesus. The prophet who proclaimed it was eliminated, crucified outside the city gate—in other words, outside human society, as the Letter to the Hebrews puts it (Heb 13:12).

But the dream continues and never died, nor will it ever die in history and in the life of Jesus's followers. There was an anticipation of the Kingdom in the resurrection of Jesus. It represents, in his person, the bursting in of a new being and of a new heaven and a new earth.

We Can All Be Christ in Our Own Way

This final reflection is a natural derivation of the incarnation of the Son of God in our human situation. The theological tradition, especially that of St. Bonaventure and Duns Scotus, has always insisted that a human being is *capax infiniti*, in other words, that human beings are capable of receiving the infinite within themselves. If we were not, the incarnation of Jesus as a human being would have been impossible.

But Jesus is truly human, as the Council of Chalcedon stated as a dogma in 451. As a human being, he is our brother. The ability of receiving the infinite in himself was in him; and, because we have the same human nature as he has and are his brothers and sisters, that ability is also in us. We are also *capax infiniti*, able to receive infinity.

Theology has always argued that a human being's salvation only takes place in absolute and definitive form when the capacities and potential hidden in them are revealed and totally realized, in the afterlife or the culmination of history. Without this supreme humanization human beings would remain incomplete and unfulfilled for all eternity.

The theological tradition coined the following words: "God, through his Son, became human so that human beings, with the same nature as Jesus, might become God." In other words, the ultimate perfection and supreme happiness of a human being, man or woman, is also to be, each in their own way and in their own measure, Christ. They see realized in themselves that capacity to receive the infinite, that is, the Son of God, becoming his brothers and sisters and sharing his destiny, that of the Kingdom of the Trinity. Mystics have said, with St. John of the Cross, "the soul becomes God by participation," through the Son of God.

Before this future reserved for us, we keep silence in reverence and gratitude to the Most Holy Trinity, which will take us into its bosom as sharers in its divine nature.

5

The Holy Spirit, Giver of Life, and the Feminine Element

Discussing the Holy Spirit is particularly important and even explosive. Heir to Greek philosophy, especially its metaphysics, classical theology, which is still dominant, was developed within the ideas of that culture, using the categories of essence, substance, and nature. These concepts, at first glance, seem static, and that was the way in which Trinity God was understood (one nature and three persons), or as one divine substance subsisting in three persons; and grace, the sacraments, the church, the priestly character, and the hierarchy were understood in the same way.

Now thinking about the Holy Spirit forces us to adopt other categories drawn from the life sciences and the universe. This brings us to a new paradigm: life, movement, process, the emergence of new and surprising things, relationships of interdependence of everyone with everyone else, history and becoming.

In other words, this way of thinking has affinities with the view of the new biology, cosmology, and astrophysics. One of the founders of quantum physics, Werner Heisenberg (1901–1976), put it like this: "The universe is not made of things but of networks of energy that can vibrate, which emerge from something deeper and more subtle." He was referring to Basic Energy, the Generative Principle of all beings.

The new story of the universe sees it in permanent genesis, expanding, creating itself, and organizing itself. Everything is emerging from a bottomless reserve of powerful and loving Energy that has been there before everything, at zero time and space. This is what sustains the Earth, every being and ourselves, crossing the whole universe from end to end of its area, which we do not know.

When we say in the creed, "I believe in the Spirit, Lord and giver of life," we are taken on to this level of representation of energy and movement, characteristic of the life phenomenon.

The Holy Spirit Fills and Moves the Universe

The *ruah* ('Spirit" in Hebrew) was already present at the first moment of creation. Over the original chaos (*tohu wabohu*), the primordial waters "blew the Spirit (*ruah*), a rush of energy" (Gen 1:2). It created all beings, animate and inanimate, especially human beings: "He breathed into his nostrils the *ruah* of life, the spirit, and he became a living being" (Gen 2:7).

The most explicit connection of the Spirit with life appears in the prophet Ezekiel, when the dry bones are covered with flesh and come to life (Ezek 37). The Spirit moves the course of the stars in their order and harmony, as is celebrated in many psalms (Ps 8). It is the Spirit that sparks the prophets' anger against the opulent who oppress the poor. At the same time, the Spirit also acts in the poetry and courage of Samson and the young David (Judg 14:6; 1 Sam 16:13).

The Spirit activates and sustains the universe in being and governs the movements of the stars. From it come the harmony and grandeur of the cosmos. It fills everything and accompanies every movement of matter and life. Nothing is beyond its reach: "Where can I go from your Spirit? Or where can I flee from your presence? (Ps 139:7).

Just as the Risen One fills the whole universe—the cosmic Christ—so the Spirit operates in the cosmogenic process until it brings it to completion.

A saying from the primitive church shows that at that time there was an awareness of the ubiquity of the Spirit: "The Spirit sleeps in the stone, dreams in the flower, awakens in the animals and knows that it is awake in human beings." I would add, "and feels that it is awake in women," since women are more similar to the Spirit because, like it, they are generators of life and so feel within themselves and do not just know in their heads.

The Messiah in particular will be "strong in the Spirit" and will appear wreathed in all the gifts of the Spirit (Isa 11:1-5).

Jesus and the Holy Spirit

Jesus bursts onto the scene as the main bearer of the Spirit. He is more than a charismatic who is sporadically seized by the Spirit. Jesus lives in the Spirit and acts through the Spirit that is in him. The very incarnation is presented as the work of the Spirit (Luke 1:35; Matt 1:20). The Spirit comes down on him at his baptism in the Jordan by John the Baptist (Mark 1:9-11; Matt 3:13-17; Luke 3:21-22; John 1:29-34). Feeling himself sent (anointed) by the Spirit, he proclaims his liberating program of curing the sick, giving sight to the blind, and freeing captives (Luke 4:18-20).

It is the Spirit that "drives" him into the desert (Mark 1:12), and from there he returns "in the power of the Spirit" (Luke 4:14). Jesus realizes that the actions that liberate humanity from its state of suffering are the product of the power (*exousia*) of the Spirit, and reveals it explicitly: "But if it is by the Spirit of God that I cast out demons, then the Kingdom of God has come to you" (Matt 12:28).

This power of the Spirit was revealed fully in the resurrection of Jesus. The Jesus according to the flesh is now seen totally transfigured into a "spiritual body" (1 Cor 15:44). In other words, the situation of the flesh, weak and limited, is now infinitely surpassed, and the historical Jesus risen takes on divine characteristics and those of the Spirit. The explosive arrival of the new human being, the risen Jesus, is an anticipation of the good end that awaits all of us and the creation of which we are a part.

This is the basis of the later Christology, which completes the earlier Jesuology.

The Holy Spirit, the Community, and the Poor

There is a deep relationship between Jesus and the Spirit, especially after the resurrection. It is the Spirit that maintains and permanently awakens the legacy of Jesus, especially for St. Paul. The symbolic story of Pentecost, in which the Spirit comes in the form of tongues of fire on all those present, from a huge variety of origins, shows the new community that is arising here, because all hear the same message in their own language (Acts 2:5–12).

In the controversy about whether circumcision should be maintained as an obligation for non-Jews who converted, the apostles appealed to the Holy Spirit and said: "It has seemed good to the Holy Spirit and to us to impose on you no further burden than these essentials" (Acts 15:28).

The Holy Spirit suggests a new organization of the Christian community, not with a hierarchy, as is the dominant model today (Petrine), but fortified by a plurality of gifts and charisms (Pauline; see 1 Cor 12:4–11).

In Paul's view, charisms are not exceptional talents but services for the community: the services of compassion and exhortation (Rom 12:8), care for the poor, and other works that cater to the structural needs of the whole community, such as teaching, leading, discerning spirits (1 Cor 12:10; Eph 4:11; Rom 12:8). The presbyter is not the person who accumulates powers but the person who has the service of concern for the cohesion and unity of the community. His task is not to concentrate power but to ensure that the charisms/services operate so that all have their role in the community.

There is a simultaneity of charisms, since all have their source in the Spirit. Hence the warning to treat as of equal worth both the more modest services and those that carry greater responsibility. The permanent warning is: "Do not quench the Spirit" (1 Thess 5:19).

Where would the church be without the community helpers, those who sing and play an instrument, those who have the gift of public speaking and can explain the Gospel texts, and others who care for the sick and comfort them? It would be a sad and tearful group of people. The *norma normans*, the supreme rule, is: "Do not seek your own advantage, but that of the other" (1 Cor 12:7), or, put in different words: "To each is given the manifestation of the Spirit for the common good" (1 Cor 12:7).

This model from the earliest days, in the Pauline communities, did not become the main one in the church; instead the hierarchical model—bishop-priest-lay person—became dominant, taking its structure and titles from the Roman imperial authorities. The category that gives cohesion is *sacra potestas*, sacred power, remote from the dream of Jesus, for whom all power is service. It is not hierarchy (sacred power), but *hierodoulia*, sacred service.

What is dominant in the church today is charism and power, and power is given more importance than charism, which makes the church a community of unequals, that is, some who hold the word and sacrament (power) and others whose task is to listen, receive the sacraments, and follow the decisions of the ecclesiastical authorities.

Our proposal is not "power or charism" but "charism and power combined." But it is on the basis of charism, of the presence of the Spirit, that power should be regulated, always in the service of the community, and not simply an

isolated office or above the community. In this power structure, those in whom charism is dominant, such as innova-
tors, creative theologians, and especially the mystics, will
always be under the harsh supervision of the bearers of
sacred power. Not infrequently, many have been isolated,
persecuted, or silenced, such as Meister Eckhart, St. John of
the Cross, Pierre Teilhard de Chardin, Yves Congar, Henri
de Lubac, Marie-Dominique Chenu, and others.

There is also a connection between the Spirit and the poor.
A famous liturgical hymn rightly calls him *Pater pauperum*,
"father of the poor." The poor are those who have the least
life. The Spirit, who is giver of life, is concerned with the
situation of these poor people. It is through the power of
the Spirit that they endure all sorts of want, illness, hunger,
and discrimination. For centuries they were made invisible,
simply an echo of the voices of others.

More recently, however, throughout the world the poor
are intruding with their organizations, especially those from
rural communities such as *Via Campesina* and the Brazilian
Landless Movement and others from various social contexts
such as the homeless movement and pressure groups for
education and health care. Especially women, in the power
of the Spirit, are demanding their right of citizenship in the
church, which is more or less denied to them.

All these movements are beginning to have a voice of
their own and to put forward their own idea of a society
that is more equal, more just, more welcoming, and more
respectful of differences of gender and sexual identity. Men
and women are no longer afraid. They are experiencing
what it is like to be free. Fearless, they take on abuse, persecution, violence, and even imprisonment, torture, exile, and
the murder of their comrades.

All this courage, apart from its significance for politics
and liberation, represents the power of the Holy Spirit that
sustains them in struggle and hope.

The Holy Spirit, Mary, and the Feminine

The supreme work of the Holy Spirit is in the unique relationship with Miriam of Nazareth. We have already touched on this. We emphasized that the first Divine Person who came to live among us was not the Son of the Father, but the Spirit of the Father and the Son. Without his coming and Mary's consent, there would never have been an incarnation.

We know that God created human beings "in his image, in the image of God he created them; male and female he created them" (Gen 1:27).

In Jesus the masculine was made divine by the Son of God. It was also appropriate that the feminine should be made explicitly divine so that there should be a balance in the design of the Trinity. And the biblical text of St. Luke says clearly that the Spirit, the third person of the Trinity, descended on Miriam of Nazareth and overshadowed her. We can connect that text with the inference of St. John, in which the Word became flesh, and, like a Bedouin, pitched his tent permanently over her (John 1:14).

The Spirit, in Hebrew and Syriac, is feminine. Miriam of Nazareth reveals a connaturality with the Holy Spirit. The evangelist Luke uses the image of a tent (*skēnē* = *episkiasei*). This expression is also used by the evangelist John to express the incarnation of the second person in the man Jesus (*skēnē* = *eskēnōsen*).

With these words Luke wanted to draw attention to the Spirit's act of spiritualization in Miriam: she was raised to the level of divinity by the Holy Spirit. "Therefore (*dio*)," says Luke the evangelist, "the child to be born of you will be holy; he will be called Son of God" (Luke 1:35). Someone can only be Son of God if they were born of someone who was adopted by the Holy Spirit, who is God.

And this someone is the one who is "blessed among all women," Mary of Nazareth. All women, not just Mary, are called to this divinization, because all are bearers of this possibility of receiving the Spirit in themselves. This possibility will, one day, be fully realized. If this were not the case, there would be an eternal void in their existence as women. Therefore every women, in her own way, will be eternally united to the Holy Spirit, and the feminine will enter into the heart of the Trinity.

Miriam of Nazareth is an advance model of what will be the reality for all women. She represents the individual realization of this universal revelation. Through her we gain the awareness that the feminine was made divine together with the masculine.

Animus and *anima*, masculine and feminine, are characteristics of every human person. In each, in different proportions (that is why there are men and women), there is the presence of the *anima* (feminine) and simultaneously of the *animus* (masculine). The feminine, divinized explicitly in Mary, bears with it an implicit divinization also of the masculine, which is also present in it. The masculine was divinized by the incarnation of the Son of the Father in Jesus of Nazareth and implicitly by the female element that is also in him. It was appropriate that the feminine should also be made divine.

Using the terminology of the medieval age and applying it to Mary (*Deus potuit, decet, ergo fecit*), God could do it, it was appropriate, and so he made divine the feminine explicitly present in Mary.

This divinization of the feminine is not merely a facet of Christianity; the great spiritual and religious traditions assert the same blessed event using other cultural codes. This understanding has not yet penetrated the official awareness of the Christian churches—which are marked by the patriarchal paradigm—but was always present in the main bearers of the spiritual heritage of Christianity, that is, the Christian people and the mystics.

In this way we reach a perfect human-divine balance. Human beings, in their unity and difference, are part of the mystery of God through the Son of the Father and through the Holy Spirit. We shall no longer be able to talk of Trinity God without talking of man and woman. We shall no longer be able to talk of man and woman without talking of Trinity God.

The offer of full meaning for women remains open. My hope is that, as C. G. Jung showed, Mary will be adored as God the Mother by the faithful, and that this assertion will become part of the awareness of Christians, women and men. Perhaps, one day, it will become the official doctrine of the Catholic Christian faith.

Jesus's purpose is to proclaim a dream, the Kingdom of God. It is the absolute revolution that transforms all things and aligns them with the plan of the Mystery. So anyone who is sick is cured, anyone who is lost finds their bearings again, anyone who has sinned against God knows mercy. Even the wind and the sea obey him. He displays power over the shadowy dimensions of existence: sickness, despair, and death. In him things begin to be renewed; the Kingdom came close and started a process that will not end until all things are transfigured.

But a tragedy is following him. "He came to what was his own, and his own people did not accept him" (John 1:11). What he offered was too new and required radical changes; he was involved in dangerous confrontations with the religious and imperial authorities, who brought him to the most shameful punishment that could be inflicted on a person, crucifixion. He did not die—he was killed. Acceptance of judicial murder was not easy for him, because it implied that his dream would not come true. That is why we hear his desperate cry on the cross: "*Eloi, Eloi, lema sabachthani?*," "My God, my God, why have you forsaken me?" (Mark 15:34). Even so, he strips himself totally of himself, of his faith and his hope. He surrenders himself to the nameless Mystery: "Father, into your hands I commend my spirit" (Luke 23:46).

But God did not forsake him. He brought to pass in his

person the dream of the Kingdom of God: he raised him from the dead. But it is a resurrection that was limited to himself without affecting humanity and creation, which still continue in the old order. In the resurrection we are given a convincing sign that the dream is not in vain and that it continues in the form of hope and historical process. The one who rose is a failure, cut to pieces by torture and disfigured by crucifixion. In other words, the Kingdom and the new world begin to be established by all those who share in the painful fate of Jesus. They are his brothers and sisters in suffering and will be the first to share in his new life.

The resurrection is personal, but because the Risen One is part of the universe, it acquires a cosmic dimension: all the elements of the universe are touched by this beginning of transfiguration. It is the beginning of a revolution in evolution. But it is only the beginning; the future is still open. The incarnate Son, limited to the space of Palestine, became through the resurrection the cosmic Christ, filling all the spaces of the universe. Saint Paul, with enthusiasm and undeniable exaggeration, was to say that he is *ta panta kai en pasin*, "all and in all" (Col 3:11). The universe bears within itself a most powerful energy that animates, brings cohesion and synthesis, and this is the risen Christ. The Kingdom which was very near, and which is in our midst, shows, seminally and initially, its action in the presence of Jesus.

6

The Church: Charism and Power, and the People of God

First and foremost, we need to emphasize that Jesus's original intention was not to found a church but to proclaim and anticipate the Kingdom of God, his great dream.

With his execution on the cross and resurrection, the Kingdom was anticipated only in his person when he was raised from the dead and burst onto the scene as the new human being, transfigured, showing what all of us will one day be. Consequently we have to distinguish between the Kingdom of God and what took its place, the church.

The Kingdom of God and the Church Are Not Identical

In the evangelists Mark, Luke, and John the word "church" does not even occur. At a late stage, when Jesus's tragic end had been assimilated and Christian communities had been formed, in the AD 90s, the evangelist Matthew turned up with this word "church," so some sixty years after Jesus's crucifixion. He connected the church with Peter's faith in Jesus as Son of God. Let it be clear: the church, according to St. Matthew, is not founded on the person of Peter but on Peter's faith. This understanding was common to both the Eastern and Western churches until at least the fourth century. It is important to note this to relativize the official interpretation of the later church institution, which sought to justify itself by succession to the apostle Peter.

Peter's merit was that before the other apostles he made the profession of faith in Jesus as Son of God (Matt 16:18). It is on this *faith*, and not on *the figure of Peter*, whom Jesus later dismissed as "Satan," that the Christian community would be built, the community of those who believe as Peter believed. But when he misunderstood the concept of "Son of God," which did not imply power and glory but abasement and the cross, Peter was sternly rebuked with the harshest expression Jesus ever used: "Get behind me, Satan! You are a stumbling block to me" (Matt 16:23).

The church only has a place because the Kingdom could not be definitively established and because there was a base to support it, *Peter's faith*. The Kingdom is the end; the church is the means. The Kingdom is the whole; the church is a part. The Kingdom is the substance; the church is its sacrament or sign to the degree that it makes visible the content of what the kingdom of God is meant to be and tries to anticipate it in the world.

The Kingdom becomes present always and wherever people live in love, solidarity, forgiveness, mercy, and a humble acceptance of God. The Kingdom therefore has a universal dimension and is established where such values are lived. The Kingdom will remain; the church will disappear.

The greatest benefit of the church, however, is to preserve the sacred memory of Jesus, not to let his dream die, create the conditions to anticipate it in history. But the church shares in the situation of sin and grace that permeates history. It is holy and sinful or, as it was even called in the first centuries, *casta meretrix*, a chaste whore: chaste when it follows the gospel, a whore when it betrays it.

Christianity as a Movement and a Spiritual Path

Christianity presented itself primarily as a movement and a path (*hodos tou Christou*). It is prior to the sediment it left in the Gospels, doctrines, rites, and churches that appeared

fifty to sixty years after the crucifixion of Christ. The movement and spiritual-way character has always remained
throughout history.

It is a type of Christianity that follows its own course.
Generally it lives on the edge of, and sometimes at a critical
distance from, the church or the churches. But it comes into
being and is nurtured by the permanent fascination with the
figure and historical saga of Jesus of Nazareth. Initially it
was regarded as "the heresy of the Nazarenes" (Acts 24:5: the
Greek word is *hairesis,* translated as "sect" in most versions;
see Acts 28:22), which means a small group, which is what it
in fact was.

But slowly it spread, especially among the poor, slaves,
and people in the poor districts of the cities of the Roman
Empire. We should never forget the humble origins of Christianity, in contrast to the Renaissance pomp of the popes
and the elaborate dress of cardinals and bishops, which has
lasted to our own time.

Christianity, however, gradually gained autonomy until
its followers were called "Christians," as the Acts of the
Apostles attests (11:26). The Jesus movement is certainly the
most important force in Christianity because it is not slotted
into institutions or imprisoned in doctrines and dogmas.

It is made up of all sorts of people, from the most diverse
cultures and spiritual traditions, even including agnostics
and atheists who find themselves fascinated by his courageous figure, by his libertarian spirit, by his message of deep
humanism, by his ethic of unconditional love, and by the
way he took on the drama of human destiny, undergoing
humiliations, torture, and execution on the cross. He presented an image of Abba God (Dear Daddy), so intimate
and life-affirming that even a person who has difficulty in
believing in God finds it hard to reject it.

Many people like this go as far as saying, "If there is a
God, it must be the one that Jesus described." Jesus has no
enemies; everyone feels attracted and close to his ideas and

way of life. The Jesus movement has the look of an elevated form of spiritual life and reveals a belief in the value of the human person, including its transcendent dimension, which is open to Someone greater.

The Pauline Dimension (Charism) and the Petrine Dimension (Power)

The Jesus movement began to get organized. Initially it was formed of meetings in family homes. Subsequently, small local communities grew up. As the number of Christians increased, there was a need for links between the different communities, some Jewish and others across the vast area of the Roman Empire.

It was then that two basic models of organizing believers crystallized. One was a community of equals, all taking part in meeting the needs of the church (charisms), as we have described before and don't need to repeat. This is the Pauline moment of the church, brothers and sisters, helping each other, flexible and attentive to changes according to the culture in which they were located, whether in Asia Minor or in Greco-Latin culture or Germanic culture. The dominant element here is charism—the source of creativity, of openness to the new, and the courage to invent in order to ensure that the Christian faith always had a Jesuanic and humanitarian face.

The second form of organization is the Petrine form. Peter, who was the first to bear witness to faith in Jesus as Son of God, is its guarantor. This form preserves the traditions, the hierarchy, and the various service roles, and began to give more importance to the bishops and presbyters than to the community of the faithful. Although the community aspect of the church never disappeared (it generally moved to monasteries, convents, and male and female religious orders), it did not become the dominant model in the church.

Through historical circumstances alien to its own nature, the Petrine church was called on to exercise political power in the Roman Empire, which was already in an advanced stage of decline. This process began in 325 with the emperor Constantine; and Christianity was officially established as a politico-religious institution in 392, when Theodosius the Great (347–395) imposed Christianity as the sole official religion of the empire. When the Byzantine emperor Justinian I (483–565), who united East and West, reconquered North Africa and also produced the first law code based on the Christian faith, the Code of Justinian (529), Christianity was made obligatory for all.

The other religions were persecuted, banned, and even eliminated. The persecuted became persecutors: the martyrs of one side produced martyrs on the other. From this point the Petrine model of a church-society organized in a hierarchy took over this power with all the titles, honors, and courtly practices that have lasted to today in the lifestyle of the ecclesiastical body.

This system frequently scandalizes believers who have read the Gospels, where they discovered the man from Nazareth, poor and humble, close to the people and remote from palaces and temples. It is the price power demands, keeping the poor at a distance and keeping close to the rich.

With Pope Francis there has been a historic shift, whose consequences only the future will show. He abandoned the papal palace and went to live in a clergy hostel, where he meets and shares meals with the other clergy. He has stripped off the high-sounding titles that came from pagan and imperial times and styles himself simply "Francis, bishop of Rome," and "inspirer of the whole universal church."

The key category that determines the structure of the Roman Church with its Petrine base is sacred power (*sacra potestas*). This power is hierarchical, exercised by a special corps, the clergy, headed by the pope, the supreme holder of sacred power.

Over time this power became ever more centralized, and showed totalitarian and even despotic tendencies—especially with Pope Gregory VII in 1075 in his *Dictatus Papae* (a good translation would be "The Dictatorship of the Pope"), who proclaimed himself absolute lord of the church and the secular world, attempting to subject kings and emperors to his will, appointing and deposing them.

Pope Boniface VIII was to give this tendency a more radical form with the bull *Unam Sanctam* (1302), in which he declared papal supremacy over princes and kings, and over all creatures. Following the same radical tendency, Innocent III (1198–1216), the most powerful pope in history—the whole of Europe as far as Russia was under his control—presented himself not merely as the successor of Peter, but as the representative of Christ.

His successor, Innocent IV (1243–1254), took the final step and proclaimed himself God's representative and so universal lord of the earth, able to distribute areas to whomever he wished, as did Popes Nicholas V (1447–1455) with Portugal in the bull *Romanus Pontifex*, and Alexander VI (1492–1503) for the kings of Spain with the bull *Inter Caetera*. This was later confirmed by the Treaty of Tordesillas, when the two monarchs divided Latin America between Portugal and Spain, a division still in effect today.

All that remained was to proclaim the infallibility of the pope, which happened at the First Vatican Council under Pius IX in 1870. The pope was credited with absolute power: "supreme, full, immediate, and universal ordinary power" (Canon 331), attributes that in fact belong only to God. Not without reason have some theologians, succubi of the popes, called the pope "a lesser God on earth." The hubris of sacred power here reached a peak beyond which it cannot rise. The poor and powerless man raised naked on the cross, the historical Jesus of Nazareth, would never have imagined such a distancing from his gospel message.

Power as Service in Jesus and as Control in the Petrine-Roman Model of the Church

Since the subject is power, it is relevant to compare the two attitudes, that of Jesus and that of the Petrine model—today the Roman Catholic Church—as regards power.

They are opposites. The evangelists present power in the form of the three temptations with which the devil confronted Jesus (Mark 1:12-13; Matt 4:1-11; Luke 4:1-13). They are placed right at the beginning, before Jesus's preaching, as a sort of entrance so that the listeners understand the master's message correctly. He is the Messiah, yes, but different, without power, turned into a suffering servant, a victim of crucifixion.

Jesus's temptations illustrate the three classical forms of power: the prophetic, which turns stones into bread, the priestly, which carries out a moral reform from the temple, and the political, which dominates peoples and creates empires.

Jesus is confronted with these powers, presented to him by Satan as projects to be taken up. Jesus rejects each of these powers. His path is not that of the Messiah whom everyone was expecting—the bearer of all these powers—but of the suffering servant and the persecuted prophet—foretold long before by the prophet Isaiah (Isa 53). This is the fundamental core of the Gospels' preaching.

With the church, the great Petrine institution, exactly the opposite occurred. Also confronted with these three temptations, it was unable to resist and succumbed thunderously to all of them. It claimed the prophetic power of the exclusive voice of the authorities and the judge of miracles, priestly power, exercised in a centralized way in the figure of the pope and distributed to the clerical corps to the complete exclusion of lay people, and political power, practiced in a monarchical and absolutist form.

This occurred especially when the popes, for centuries,

had in their hands all power, secular and religious, and ran a papal state, with its bureaucracy, its central bank, armies, and even a judicial system that sentenced people to death.

In its basic structure, this type of Petrine organization remains in existence down to today, with all the contradictions it involves. It has difficulty in avoiding the charge Jesus made against Peter, who did not understand Jesus's path of humility and humiliation: Jesus called him "Satan" and "a stumbling block" (Matt 16:23).

The rock of the present Vatican palaces is certainly not the base on which Jesus would have built his church. The price that has to be paid by an institutional church that bases itself on power is to live in permanent disputes, conflicts, crusades, and wars with other powermongers, now allied with them, now pulling them down from their thrones and excommunicating them—very much in the logic Hobbes describes in his *Leviathan*: "Power always wants more power because it cannot guarantee its power without seeking more and more power."

A church institution based on Petrine power tends to close the doors to love and easily loses the poor. An ally of the powerful, it becomes incapable of evangelizing the poor and denouncing the causes of their poverty; it reduces them to consumers of religious benefits, submissive and without any participation in the decisions that affect the life and organization of the church. The institution loses its human face and becomes insensitive to existential problems, often being cruel and merciless in the face of problems connected with doctrine, the family, and sexuality.

In the various aspects of present-day culture, this type of Petrine institutional church has transformed itself into a bastion of authoritarianism, conservatism, and machismo, increasingly distant from the way the world is going and increasingly unable to establish a frank and open dialogue with the modern world, with its various freedoms, with democracy, or with any worlds beyond its own.

Its institutional arrogance in claiming to be the exclusive bearer and legitimate interpreter of revelation, the only true church of Christ, denying to all other churches, except the Orthodox, the title of church (we need only look at Cardinal Josef Ratzinger's 2000 doctrinal document *Dominus Jesus*), presenting itself as the exclusive bearer of the means of salvation to the extent of repeating the medieval slogan "Outside the church no salvation," is making it increasingly unacceptable to sensible and ecumenically minded people, with the risk of turning itself into a great Western Christian sect.

Thanks to the Spirit, someone was elected pope who is outside the parameters of European Petrine Christianity, which is in its death throes and incapable of being a source of meaning for the future of the Earth and of humanity. Pope Francis wants a church that goes out to the world, especially to socially and existentially deprived areas.

Francis clearly has two passions: (1) a passion for the historical Jesus, whose life he constantly urges us to imitate in his preaching, and (2) an existential encounter with him and a passion for the poor and most vulnerable of this world— he denounces those responsible for their oppression with a clarity and courage unheard of in previous pontificates.

His model is a church that is a "field hospital" serving all, with little concern for their religious affiliation or moral situation. It is a church that expressly gives center stage to mercy and tenderness, banishing all the fear that was always the main element in traditional evangelization.

He emphasizes that for God there is no such thing as eternal condemnation, since apart from the justice that will be applied (a spell in God's hospital), the main approach will be one of infinite mercy, according to the Jesus of the Gospels and the famous passage of Psalm 103: "He will not always accuse. . . . He does not deal with us according to our sins. . . . For he knows how we were made; he remembers that we are dust. But the steadfast love of the Lord is from everlasting to everlasting" (Ps 103:9, 14, 17).

The predominant model of church here is different: a church of service, prophetic, ecumenical, and deeply concerned about the future of the Common Home and nature, as revealed in Francis's exceptional encyclical *Laudato Si': On Care for Our Common Home* (2015). A theological term has been coined to describe the rise of a church at the grass roots through the power of God's Spirit. The term is "ecclesiogenesis," the birth of a new type of church. This term went round the world and was incorporated into general theological discourse.

To end this section we should stress that the historical Petrine and Pauline churches always competed as two possible models. It is not a question of the church as either charism and power but of the church as charism and power, as I tried to explain in my 1982 book of the same title that was censured because it was misinterpreted as a church of either charism or power. That is not what I argued or wrote. I maintained, and still maintain, that in the church there is power and there is charism, but charism and power have to interact correctly. Both are attributes of the church. The charism that comes from the Spirit should regulate and limit the power and strive for it to be exercised as service, in the sense that Jesus taught.

The Church as the People of God: The Church Base Communities and Ecclesiogenesis

Alongside the official version of Christianity incarnate in Greco-Latin erudite culture, there came into being from the beginning a vigorous popular Christianity.

The Christianity of Popular Culture

The Christianity of popular culture is not a degenerate form of the official version. On the contrary, it possesses the same dignity but incarnates the message of Jesus in the worldview of ordinary people. Here it is not the *logos*, reason, but *pathos, the heart and deep feeling*, that organizes the words. It is expressed in the language of the imagination, the heart, and affection.

It possesses its own truths and its own way of putting things, of praying to God and living the dream of Jesus. It has its own feasts, its own favorite saints, and nurtures a deep and simple faith. This ordinary people's Christianity has been almost always despised and treated as mere lumpen religion, to be ruled by the doctrines and rites of the clerical elite. Nevertheless, without confrontation or conflict with the official, Petrine model, it created its own path and developed a Christianity of everyday life, of personal and family virtues, of following Jesus, generally the crucified Jesus, in whom people saw their own situation of crucifixion. This is a real ecclesiogenesis, the birth of a church reflecting the faith of the people.

These anonymous believers kept the secret of Jesus's dream, a mixture of hope, many virtues, and a trusting surrender to God's will. Far from power, they did not suffer the pathologies typical of the powerful: double standards, pharisaism, hypocrisy, hardheartedness, arrogance, and the vanity that delights in ostentation. They live a pure and simple Christianity as authentic heirs of Jesus's ethic and his dream, of a world where the benefits of the Kingdom begin to appear, and we have a foretaste of the divine promises.

Saint Joseph is the patron of the anonymous believers, the voiceless, the simple men and women lay faithful inspired by the words and actions of Jesus. Like everything else, this type of Christianity has its limitations and mistakes. Quite often it mixes faith with superstitions and produces strange mixtures, and it too easily treats as supernatural things that are simply natural. But just as illnesses remind us of health, these deviations derive from the healthy substance of Jesus's gospel, with all it has to offer of hope, happiness, and celebration. Popular Christianity is festive, surrounded by patron saints, full of color, dancing, drink, and lots of food.

In more general terms, and in the jargon of the new cosmology, we have to say that Christianity is an emergence of the universe based on the premise of the failure of the crucified historical Jesus. Everything was rearranged so that Jesus's cause and the meaning of his achievements could be perpetuated in history in various styles of expression.

The rise of the Jesus movement, the writing of the four Gospels, the foundation of communities within Judaism and Hellenism, the spread of the magic of the figure and message of Jesus across the lives of millions of people—in art, music, and written and virtual literature down to our own time—show the action of Basic Energy and the Christic energies of ascension acting in history.

All this certainly escaped whatever awareness the historical Jesus had, as a child of his time. That doesn't matter. It was God who, through him, brought about this emergence in our cosmic, earthly, and human history.

Christianity only has meaning if it keeps alive the awareness that it is an emergence based on the presence of the creator Spirit, the Father's Son, and the Father himself in our midst. It acquires relevance to the extent that it does not allow Jesus's dream to cool, if it keeps alive the memory of his words and actions, his glorious and tragic achievements, if it attempts to make the dream real in what are called the benefits of the Kingdom, made up of love, mercy, forgiveness, care for the poor and for the Common Home, and totally surrender to the Daddy God, as though we feel ourselves in the palm of his hand. But Christianity is relevant principally, if we feel ourselves to be really sons and daughters of the Father by the power of the Holy Spirit and pass on this surpassing dignity to all.

We are of God and belong to God's family. Why should we be afraid? Christians, for good or ill, carry forward this

mission in the midst of many contradictions and with difficult fidelities and burdensome betrayals. But they always
press on and never give up believing and hoping that Jesus's
dream can and will come true. The future of humanity, of
the world and the universe is in the Kingdom of God, which
is the Kingdom of the Trinity.

The power of Christianity does not reside in doctrines
and faithfulness to traditions, which are always human
creations, but in hope against all hopes and in a spirituality, as Pope Francis emphasizes in his ecological encyclical,
that "can motivate us to a more passionate concern for the
protection of our world. A commitment this lofty cannot be
sustained by doctrine alone, without a spirituality capable
of inspiring us, without an "interior impulse which encourages, motivates, nourishes and gives meaning to our individual and communal activity" (*Laudato Si'*, §216). Then
there will be only the love and celebration of free people, in
a creation finally redeemed and turned into a temple where
we and the Trinity God will live forever and ever.

The Church: People of God

Popular Christianity joyfully adopted the understanding
of the church as People of God, given such emphasis by
the Second Vatican Council (1962–1965) in chapter 2 of its
Dogmatic Constitution on the Church, *Lumen Gentium*. In
the first place it has a sense of universality; in other words,
everyone belongs to the People of God, as stated in the first
paragraph: "At all times and in every race God has given
welcome to whosoever fears Him and does what is right" (9,
referencing Acts 10:35).

The People of God come first, before the hierarchical
structure of the church. Vatican II changed the order of the
draft text, in which the chapter "The Hierarchical Structure
of the Church" came first, and only afterward the chapter on
the "People of God." This switch is very important because

it gives the People of God priority over the hierarchical structure, which becomes a function of service to the People of God. The whole church, clergy and laity, are the People of God. The category People of God has the advantage of including all the faithful prior to any internal differentiation (clergy and laity). It integrates the common priesthood and the ministerial priesthood into the one priesthood of Christ (LG 10).

In addition, the category People of God gives the church a historical character, an open construction as it journeys through time in the company of other peoples who are also journeying toward God. In other words, it retrieves the biblical dimension of the church with its perspective of covenant and mission.

Although it is the baptized who form the messianic People of God, all peoples, in some way, are the People of God, because they are under the rainbow of divine grace (LG 9, 13). With different densities, the People of God is also a reality among non-Catholic Christians and in world religions; even atheists who have goodwill, who live a good life, are not beyond its reach (LG 16).

In this perspective, the People of God can be taken to mean all those who have in them the presence of the Spirit and the Risen One and divine grace, though at different levels of insertion into the reality of what we call "the church" (LG 14–16). We might think that the redeemed humanity that welcomes God in communion through a just life would constitute the People of God in the wider sense.

To put this train of thought more formally, on the basis of Vatican II, we can say that humanity as a whole forms the People of God to the extent that it is open to divine visitation. The church in its historical institutionality can be described as the sacrament (sign and instrument) of the People of God and will emerge as the messianic People of God.

Vatican II's whole conception of the People of God is permeated by the demand that all the faithful should share and have communion in Christ's service as prophet, priest, and king (LG 10–12), which translates into the active involvement in the various church ministries and in the charisms given for the common good (LG 12). This People of God acquires substance in the particular churches, in the church base communities, and in individual cultures, whose values and customs are taken up into this service, since the Spirit is constantly active in them (LG 13).

Despite the differences, "all share a true equality with regard to the dignity and to the activity common to all the faithful for the building up of the Body of Christ" (LG 32). The idea of the People of God lays down a demand for conscious participation, communal organization for a common project, equality among all, unity amid differences, and communion of all with all and with God. As this is a people and not an aimless and disorganized mass, there are structures of leadership and inspiration, but they come from within the People of God; they are not above it or outside it, but inside and at the service of the People of God. A church in which, for example, the laity cannot share in sacred power or in which women are in principle excluded and cannot speak in meetings, in which decisions are concentrated in the clerical caste, cannot really, except metaphorically, be called the People of God. The basic minimum of participation, equality, and communion is lacking, without which the reality of the People of God cannot come into being, and we are left with a shapeless mass of believers, customers of a center of religious services and private consumers in a market of symbolic commodities. This is not the theological basis for the church as a community of faith and the People of God.

"People of God" is a meaningful definition of the church, and not a metaphor, only if it is the result of a network of communities in which the faithful participate, allocate responsibilities to each other, and live the reality of communion.

This inclusive understanding is a break with the old idea of a Petrine society, still visible in the words of Pope Gregory XVI (1831–1846), who insisted: "No one can be unaware of the fact that the church is an unequal society, in which God has destined some to be governors, and others to be servants. The latter are the laity, and the former the clergy."

This type of ecclesiology represents the ideology of those who hold power in the church in an exclusive way; it is too narrow to create communion and participation among all the faithful, perversely reinforces the marginalization of the laity and the exclusion of women, and represents a pathological state that must be cured by a vision more in tune with Jesus's utopian idea that we are all brothers and sisters (Matt 23:8–12).

The understanding of the church as the People of God sends us back to the real, nonmetaphorical definition of the church as *communitas fidelium* (community of the faithful), and so something visible and real and not merely symbolic or metaphorical.

The church is not first and foremost a priestly body that creates communities, but the community of those who responded with faith to the call of God in Jesus through his Spirit. The network of these communities forms the People of God because this is the result of a communal, participatory process. The various functions arise from within the community, some permanent in character, such as the need to proclaim, celebrate, act in the world, and create unity among the faithful and the ministries, and so more institutionalized services come into being because they are a response to permanent needs that are better met by institutionalized functions. Others arise that are more sporadic, but equally important for maintaining the life of the communities: the service of charity, concern for the poor, the promotion of social justice, particularly human, individual, and social rights, and the rights of nature and Mother Earth.

Both charisms give life to the community and ensure that it is not only organized and has rules (Petrine) but above all is creative and radiates hope and joy, elements that are part of the gospel (Pauline).

It will be clear that this understanding of the church as community and People of God does not exclude, but includes, church hierarchy. This is a permanent charism, a real charismatic state because it meets a permanent need among the community, unity among all. But it is within the People of God and at its service and not outside it or—what can be worse—above it.

In an ecclesiology that regards the church as a hierarchical society (Petrine), there is no salvation for women in the sense of integration into community services and gifts (Pauline). They are forever marginalized, if not excluded. This state of affairs is incompatible with an ecclesiology that is minimally based on the gospel, which has to incorporate human values because they are also divine values. This is the fundamental reason why we should abandon an exclusively Petrine ecclesiology based on society and hierarchy and build up a Pauline ecclesiology, of community and the People of God.

Church Base Communities:
The Grassroots Church and Ecclesiogenesis

One embodiment of the concept of the People of God exists in poor communities. These are the church base communities, or CEBs, which have existed since the 1950s and today exist in every part of the world, including in countries that were the center of old Christendom.

Before we go any further, we need to emphasize that the CEBs are not a sort of parish ministry, like youth ministry, marriage accompaniment, or, in this case, ministry to the poor. This is a new way of being the church at the base, whether the base of the church (lay men and women) or the base of society (the poor and those who live in rural areas or the poor districts of towns).

They bring to life the original meaning of church, which is being a community of faith and People of God on a journey. They come into being from what is essential, faith in Christ who died and rose again and in the power of the Holy Spirit. In other words, they are the essential content of the church, the basics, faith lived in community.

But there is something new here: this faith creates communities among the poor, who are generally unsupported by the (Petrine) church, as a great institution. They meet under a tree or in a small hall that is also used as a school and a place for parties. The reading of the Word and discussion of it is central. A passage from the Bible is read and related to an episode from ordinary life. Through this meeting, light is shed on life, and in this light the community makes its communal decisions.

There is a lot of prayer in the communities. A hymn book has been created based on popular culture and emphasizing liberation from the community's oppressions. The principal characteristic of this new way of being the church is to be community and a family. Everyone feels like a brother or sister, and everyone takes on a different task (charism). There are the coordinators, generally women, and all the other services are allocated according to the abilities of the members. No one is left without a job.

The leaders of the CEBs are lay men and women. Priests and bishops can participate. It is not uncommon to see, for example, a cardinal seated among the people. At the end, he, with the rest of the community, receives the blessing from those who led the celebration, men and women.

Lay men and women discover that they are successors of the apostles in the sense that they feel themselves to be heirs of the apostles' teaching and responsible for the unity of all. Apostolicity is a mark of the whole church, not just of the bishops. They feel themselves to be apostles and missionaries. It is not uncommon for a more mature community to establish others and support them in their development.

The CEBs, in being communities of faith, having the Word, celebrations, and community services, constitute a real church at the grass roots, and don't just have features of the church. They may be enriched if they have a deacon or deaconess or even a priest among them, but they do not lose their lay character, because the lay men and women are their leaders.

A CEB is a force for liberation. Through following the poor man Jesus and strengthened by his Spirit, its members get involved in the defense of human rights, especially the rights of the poor, which are rights to life, to the means of life, and human dignity. Others get involved in work for social justice and become members of unions. Others again go so far as to join organizations, taking forward what they call Kingdom values—social justice starting with the least important, welcoming the weakest, defending the dignity of those who cannot defend themselves, and so on. They understand the party that stands for social justice, especially by including the poor, as one of the instruments of an incipient establishment of the Kingdom of God, the great liberating idea of the historical Jesus.

The CEBs do not just produce involved Christians but also critical citizens who identify the causes of their impoverishment, namely, the unjust social relationships that create inequality and offend God as sins against the brothers and sisters. Because of their social commitment, in some countries of Latin America they have suffered persecution, imprisonment, torture, and even assassination. They are the martyrs of the Kingdom of God. The best known is the archbishop of San Salvador, Óscar Arnulfo Romero, who was assassinated as he celebrated Mass and officially declared a saint by Pope Francis in 2018.

Together with this commitment, the CEBs never cease to celebrate the liberation brought by Christ and the presence of the Spirit, who constantly encourages them in the face of all the sufferings their social situation brings with it. These celebrations make clear the union of life and faith, because the prayers mention the battles for health care and education and denounce their oppressors, the modern pharaohs. And when a school or health center is built, or a particular road is paved after great pressure on the authorities, there are celebrations because what is associated with the Kingdom of God benefits everyone.

The CEBs are a challenge for the whole church, a challenge to be more of a community and less of a hierarchy, simpler and more like the gospel, which describes Jesus as poor and a friend of the poor, who had nowhere to lay his head, who lived far from the palaces and close to the simple dwellings of the unimportant people of this world. It is not for nothing that Pope John XXIII and especially Pope Francis have expressed the desire that the church should be a poor church and always on the side of the poor—who are privileged members of the Kingdom—those whom Jesus called "the least of these who are members of my family" (Matt 25:40).

The greater dream, in the new planetary phase of humanity, is that the whole church should consist of faith communities incarnate in different cultures, giving a new face to the eternal message of Jesus. It could have a coordination center, which could be the pope with his basic services, in communion with other Christian churches, helping humanity to reinvent itself as humanity, more just, more fraternal, and more tender, in which it would be easier to live Jesus's dream of unconditional love and waiting for the coming of the definitive Kingdom with a new heaven and a new earth.

7

Freeing Mother Earth: An Ecotheology of Liberation

Ecology, from its derivation, means thinking about (Greek *logos, logia*) the home (Greek *oikos*), about habitat, and, in a more globalizing extension, the Common Home, the Earth. The term was coined by a disciple of Charles Darwin, the German zoologist Ernst Haeckel (1834–1919).

Ecology in the Strict Sense

Haeckel defines it as follows: "It is the study of the interdependence and interaction between living organisms (animals and plants) with their (inorganic) environment." It is possible that Haeckel himself didn't realize that with this definition he'd created an intellectual revolution. Before him each science had concerned itself with a specific object, unrelated to others: rocks or plants or animals or human beings. This is the basis of modern science, fragmented and divided into its specialties.

Haeckel introduced a new element that later became the fundamental theoretical core of quantum physics: everything is related to everything else at every moment and in all circumstances. Everything is relation, and nothing exists outside a relation.

Haeckel's achievement was to have realized that science cannot cling to its analysis of its objects of knowledge in themselves, without relating them to the context in which they are situated. He realized that, for them to exist, a network of relations connects and reconnects all of them. In order to understand them, we have to understand their relations. Accordingly, for Haeckel, ecology is the science of relations, of each being with its habitat and with the other beings present.

So ecology is the science of the relations of all beings with each other, from the most distant galaxies to the ant running along my desk. They are mutually related by what supports them, gravitational energy, as well as being formed of the same elements that matured inside the great red stars over several billion years after that huge explosion we know as the Big Bang.

Such pan-relationality forms the environment, an expression created by Jakob von Uexküll (1864–1944). This idea meant that science no longer stayed inside laboratories but got organically involved with nature, in which everything lives alongside everything else, forming the vast community of life. In this vision, ecology cannot be defined in its own terms, apart from its involvement with other fields of knowledge. It is not knowledge of objects to be known but of relations between objects. It turns out to be knowledge of mutually related fields of knowledge. It is the ecologization of fields of knowledge.

This network of connections gave rise to the concept of holism (*holos* in Greek means totality). This expression was introduced by the South African general Jan Smuts to replace the reductionist view of nature as sets of objects rather than an understanding of the webs of relations that connect everything with everything else.

Life: An Essential Part of Planet Earth

One name, however, has to be mentioned because it hardly appears in ecological literature, and it is that of the Russian geochemist Vladimir Vernadsky (1863–1945). The concept of the biosphere was already in existence, and had been introduced by the Austrian Edward Suess (1831–1914), but the person who made it central and a key term in ecology was Vernadsky with his 1926 book entitled simply *Biosphere.* Vernadsky showed that life is an essential part of planet Earth, a component that transforms cosmic radiation into active earthly energy. Life cannot be understood apart from its inseparable relations with the physical and chemical phenomena that occur on the planet.

Because of this holistic understanding, Vernadsky suggested a global ecology, in other words an ecology of planet Earth as a whole and with the totality of its cosmic relationships. In this way he turned the Earth with all its ecosystems into an object of study and analysis, as later did James Lovelock with his Gaia hypothesis, which regards the Earth as a single living organism.

This idea did not gain force until relatively recently, when global phenomena such as global warming, the shortage of drinking water, the reduction of biodiversity, the desertification of vast areas of the planet, and the increasing frequency of typhoons and tsunamis forced people to think of the Earth in its totality. It made us aware of our common destiny, since we are all in the same new Noah's Ark, planet Earth, regulated by the biosphere.

Curiously, global ecology establishes an objective solidarity of human beings with all the other living creatures that also need the biosphere (water, clean air, foodstuffs, fibers, and other things) to live and go on living.

Ecology remained a sort of subchapter of biology for almost a century. This situation changed in 1972 when the Club of Rome, a group of notable scientists, economists, business leaders, and former politicians concerned with the state of the planet, commissioned a research project from the Massachusetts Institute of Technology under the direction of Professor Dennis Meadows, a study of the health of the planet, which led to the publication of *The Limits to Growth*.

The results shocked the scientists: the Earth was sick and had no antibodies to maintain its vitality. The diagnosis was correct: the Earth's sickness is due to the rapacious and consumerist type of development our societies indulge in. The result of the report was that ecology left universities and came on to the streets and became a key issue in world politics. We have to ensure the sustainability of the Common Home, without which there will be no future, not for life, not for the human species, and not for the Earth as the great living organism.

As we can see, ecology has become the central issue of all social policies, health, the atmosphere, and of all economic activity: all are judged by the degree to which they affect the environment, pollute it or preserve it, whether they guarantee the vitality and habitability of every ecosystem and of the Earth as a whole.

Before we look at the various current tendencies in ecological thinking we need to discuss two fundamental issues without which ecological understanding and practice become ineffective and just more of the same. "The thinking that created the crisis," Einstein said, "cannot be the thinking that will get us out of it." We have to look for a new cosmology that redefines our relationship with nature and the Earth. We either change or face an ecological Armageddon.

Two Cosmologies in Conflict

In the face of the systemic crisis through which the planet is going, a great debate is under way, an exchange of ideas about the future of the Earth, of life, and of our civilization. In other words, it is a great debate about the two cosmologies that are in opposition in international debate. Each projects its view of the future.

"Cosmology" means worldview, the view of the world that underlies the ideas, the activities, the habits, and dreams of a society. Every culture has its own cosmology through which it attempts to explain the origin, evolution, and purpose of the universe and define the place of the human being within it.

Our current cosmology is the cosmology of conquest, of power as domination. To use a metaphor, it is Alexander the Great's cosmology for the ancient world and that of Hernán Cortés for Amerindia. Both proved to be symbols of the desire for power and domination.

In the modern era, from the sixteenth century until today, domination of the mechanisms of nature and exploration of the world was carried out in expectation of progress and unlimited growth. Its approach is anthropocentric, mechanistic, deterministic, atomistic, and reductionist. This worldview has brought us to a situation in which less than 20 percent of the world's population controls and consumes 80 percent of all the natural resources, creating a gulf between rich and poor deeper than ever in world history.

Half of the great rain forests have been destroyed, 65 percent of cultivable land has been lost, between 27,000 and 100,000 species of living creatures disappear annually, and 100,000 synthetic chemical agents, most of them toxic, are released each year into the ground, into the air, or into water.

Weapons of mass destruction have been produced that are capable of wiping out all human life. The ultimate effect is to unbalance the Earth system, and this is expressed in global warming. With the gases already accumulated, before 2030 we shall inevitably reach an additional 2°C; and, if we do little to reduce emissions of greenhouse gases, by the end of the century we shall reach temperature increases of 4°-5°C, as a result of so-called abrupt warming, as the North American scientific community has warned. Such abrupt warming would make life as we know it today practically impossible, and the human species itself would be at risk of largely disappearing.

The predominance of economic interests, especially speculation (making money without work or production, money making money), which are able to reduce countries to the most brutal poverty and consumerism, has trivialized our perception of the risk under which we are living and has worked against any change of direction.

In opposition to this attitude, an alternative cosmology with the potential to save us is gaining strength, the cosmology of transformation and liberation. It has been developed for over a century and has been best expressed in the Earth Charter (2000) and in Pope Francis's encyclical *Laudato Si': On Care for Our Common Home* (2015). On this the Canadian cosmologist Mark Hathaway and I produced a study that took thirteen years of wide-ranging interdisciplinary scientific research, published under the title *The Tao of Liberation: Exploring the Ecology of Transformation* (2010), which was awarded the Nautilus Gold Medal for the category Cosmology and New Science.

This new cosmology is derived from the universe, Earth, and life sciences. It locates our situation within cosmogenesis, that huge process of evolution that started with the Big Bang around 13.7 billion years ago.

I have said this before, but it bears repeating: the universe is constantly in transformation, expansion, organizing itself and creating itself. Its natural state is evolution and not stability; transformation and adaptability, not immutability and permanence. In the universe, everything is relationship in networks, and nothing exists outside this relationship. As a result, all beings are interdependent and collaborate to evolve together and ensure the equilibrium of all factors. The basic concern is not to amass material goods but to sustain all life.

Transformation/liberation is part of the logic of life: a seed turns into a stem, a trunk, leaves, a canopy, flowers, and fruit. It is the same with every living organism and ourselves. We are not the same as when we were children, nor shall we be the same when we are leaving this world. Everything is transformation, especially at death, the moment of the great alchemical transition, and there is a transition to another level and a different order of life. We do not end with death; we are transformed, by death, into higher and more complex forms of life. Christians say: we do not live for death; we die to rise again, to be transformed and freed from the bonds of space and time, and from all forms of oppression, to become new men and women.

Behind all beings acts Fundamental Energy, also called the Nurturing Abyss of all being, which gave origin to the universe and keeps it in being, bringing into existence new beings. The most spectacular of these is the living Earth and we human beings with our component of consciousness and intelligence and the mission to care for the Earth.

We are living in critical times. It is now that the new cosmology shows its power to inspire: instead of dominating nature, it places nature at its heart in deep harmony and synergy. It is the paradigm created by Francis of Assisi, described by Pope Francis in his ecological encyclical: "he would call creatures, no matter how small, by the name of 'brother' or 'sister'" (*Laudato Si'*, §11). In this "Franciscan" worldview we stand erect alongside all creatures, feeling ourselves part of nature.

What characterizes this new cosmology is care instead of domination, the recognition of the intrinsic value of every being and not its mere utilization by human beings, respect for all life, and the rights and dignity of nature and not its exploitation.

The strength of this cosmology resides in the fact that it is more in accord with the real needs of human beings and with the logic of the universe itself. If we adopt it, we shall be creating the opportunity for a planetary civilization in which the life of the Earth and human beings, care, cooperation, love, respect, happiness, and spirituality occupy the central place. It will be the great saving change we urgently need.

At this point in history we need to go beyond the economic and financial aspects of the crisis and get down to its basic causes. If we don't, the causes of the crisis will carry on, producing ever more dramatic crises until they become tragedies on an unimaginable scale.

What underlies the current crisis is the breakdown of the classical cosmology that lasted for centuries but can no longer cope with the transformations that have taken place in humanity and on planet Earth. This cosmology began about five millennia ago, when the great empires began to be formed, gained strength at the Enlightenment, and has culminated in the endeavors of today's science and technology, which was harshly criticized by Pope Francis in *Laudato Si'* for being anthropocentric (treating nature as if it were at the service of humankind) and marked by hubris (the arrogant claim that we possess the key to solving all problems, when that attitude is the main cause of those problems).

This cosmology started from a mechanistic and anthropocentric vision of the universe: things are there alongside each other without connection between them, and have value only insofar as they exist to be used by human beings. Human beings think of themselves as outside and above nature, as its lord and master (*maître et possesseur*, in René Descartes's words), able to make use of it as they see fit.

It started from a false premise that we could produce and consume without limit on a limited planet. The premise also assumes that the fictitious abstraction known as money represents the highest value and that competition and the pursuit of individual interest will result in general well-being. As I described earlier, it takes the form of a cosmology of domination. This cosmology has brought the crisis into the sphere of ecology, politics, ethics, and now of economics. The eco-feminists have pointed out the close connection between anthropocentrism and patriarchy, which since Neolithic times has been doing violence to women and nature.

Earth, according to renowned cosmologists and biologists, is a living planet—Gaia—which makes physical, chemical, and biological processes work together in a way that is always beneficial to life. All its elements are made available in the right quantities so subtly that only a living organism could do this.

It is only in the last few decades, and now there can be no mistaking this, that the earth has started to show signs of stress and loss of sustainability. Both the universe and the Earth are showing themselves to be directed by a purpose that is revealed by the emergence of increasingly complex and conscious orders.

We human beings are the conscious and intelligent part of the universe and the Earth. Because we have these abilities, we can face crises, detect points of certain cultural habits (paradigms) that are ecologically harmful, and invent new ways of being human, of producing, of consuming, of living together and accepting differences. This is the cosmology of transformation/liberation, an expression of the new age, the ecozoic age.

This new worldview will certainly force us to make a qualitative leap toward a different model of production and consumption, which could indeed save us, because it would be more in harmony with the logic of life, with Gaia's cycles, and everyday human needs.

The Underlying Root of the Ecological Crisis: The Break with the Universal Attachment[1]

We are considering the historical and intellectual causes underlying the present ecological crisis. But we have to get

---

1. Trans. note: In the Portuguese the word for "attachment" is close to the word for "religion," and the text plays implicitly with this.

to the underlying cause, the permanent break of the basic attachment (one of the root meanings of the world "religion") that human beings caused, a breaking of the attachment to nature, to the Earth, to the whole of the universe, and to its Creator, which has reached a frightening pace in our own time.

Here we are touching on a profoundly mysterious and tragic dimension of human and universal history. The Judeo-Christian tradition calls this fundamental frustration the sin of the world; and theology, following St. Augustine, who coined the expression, calls it "original sin" or the original fall.

"Original" here has nothing to do with the historical origins of this anti-phenomenon, with the past. It refers to what is at the origin of human beings, what affects their radical basis and sense of being. In other words, it is about the human condition now.

Moreover, sin cannot be reduced to a mere moral dimension or a human mistake. It has to do with a globalizing attitude, that is, with the overturning of all the relationships in which human beings are a part. It concerns an ontological dimension affecting human beings, considered as a bundle of relations. This bundle is distorted and vitiated, which damages all types of relationship.

It is important to emphasize that original sin is an interpretation of a fundamental experience, a reply to a challenging puzzle. For example, there is the splendor of a cherry tree in blossom in Japan and at the same time a tsunami in Fukushima that destroys everything. There is a Mother Teresa of Calcutta, who saves people dying on the streets, and a Hitler, who sends six million Jews to the gas chambers. Why does this contradiction exist? Philosophers and theologians are still racking their brains to find an answer, and to this day they haven't found one.

Without going into the many possible interpretations, we shall adopt one, since it is gaining an increasing consensus among religious thinkers—unfulfillment as a moment in the evolutionary process. God did not create the universe as a finished object, once and for all, a past event, perfect in every way. God launched an open and perfectible process, evolution, which was to travel toward ever more complex, subtle, and perfect forms. We hope that one day it will reach its Omega Point.

Unfulfillment is not a defect but a mark of evolution. It does not reflect God's ultimate design for his creation but a moment in an immense process. The earthly paradise does not mean nostalgia for a lost golden age but the promise of a future that is still to come. The first page of the Scriptures is really the last. It comes at the beginning as a sort of model of the future so that readers may be filled with hope for the happy ending of all creation.

Saint Paul saw the fallen state of creation as subjection to "futility" (*mataiotēs*), not because of human beings but because of God himself. The exegetical sense of "futility" points to a process of maturation. Nature has not yet reached its maturity; because of this, in its current stage it is still far from the goal to be reached. So it is that "the whole creation has been groaning in labor pains until now" (Rom 8:22).

Human beings are part of this process of coming to maturity, and groaning (Rom 8:23). The whole of creation is waiting anxiously for the full maturity of the sons and daughters of God because between them and the rest of creation there is a deep interdependence and attachment. When this maturity is reached, creation will also come to its maturity, since, as Paul says, it "will share the glorious freedom of the sons and daughters of God" (Rom 8:21).

It is then that God's ultimate design will be achieved. Only then will God be able to utter the longed-for words: "he saw everything that he had made, and indeed, it was very good." For now these words are prophecies and promises for the future, because not everything is good. The philosopher Ernst Bloch (the author of *The Principle of Hope*) put it well: "Genesis is at the end, not the beginning." The delay in the coming of human beings to maturity implies a delay in creation; their advance implies an advance of the whole. It can be an instrument of liberation or an obstacle to the evolutionary process.

This is where the drama begins: when evolution reaches the human level it reaches the level of consciousness and freedom. Human beings were created to be creators. They can intervene in nature for good, to care for it, or for ill, to devastate it.

This intervention may have started, who knows, with the appearance of *homo habilis,* 2.7 million years ago, when he made the tools with which he intervened without respecting the rhythms of nature. At the beginning, it might have been one act, but repetition created an attitude of lack of care. Instead of being alongside things, living with them, human beings set themselves above them, to dominate them. And this process took on speed down to our time, this pitiless war against Gaia, with no prospect that in the end we would be victorious. Earth does not need us; it is we that need her. The last word rests with her, not with the human pretension to dominate her.

With this presumptuousness, human beings fractured the natural solidarity between all creatures, went against the design of the Creator, who had appointed them as co-creators with the mission of completing the imperfect creation with their ingenuity. But human beings put themselves in the place of God; in the power of their intelligence and will they felt themselves to be little gods, and behaved as though they were omnipotent. The modern era, with its desire for power and domination, created the God complex, thinking that it could dominate everything and, through science, solve all problems. This arrogance has now become irrational and even ridiculous; human beings do not dominate nature nor the laws of the Earth and the universe, but are dominated by them. This frustration of the idea that they were "little gods" has brought to a crisis the process of civilization and even human beings' understanding of themselves.

This is the great break with nature and the Creator that underlies the ecological crisis. The problem is not the type of human being that was produced through history, more a "geophysical force of destruction" (Edward O. Wilson) or the new geological era of the Anthropocene, than a creature that cares and preserves.

The remedy lies in restoring the link with all things. We do not necessarily need to be more religious, but it is important to be humbler, to feel part of nature, more responsible for its sustainability, and more careful in everything we do. We need to return to the Earth from which we have exiled ourselves and feel ourselves to be its guardian and carer. Then the natural contract will be remade. And if we also open ourselves to the Originating Source of all beings, we will slake our infinite thirst and receive as a reward lasting peace with ourselves and with the heart of all things.

Branches of Comprehensive Ecology

From this root reflection, and linked more directly with political and social approaches to ecology, various studies and tendencies have grown: ecology as conservation of threatened species, plant ecology, animal ecology, population ecology, environmental ecology, social ecology, deep ecology, and others.

We shall stick to four basic options since they seek to think of an integral or comprehensive ecology as suggested by Pope Francis's encyclical *Laudato Si'* and the Earth Charter adopted by UNESCO, which I helped to write.

Environmental Ecology: The Quality of Life

For quality of life to be strong it is important for air to be clean, water sources not polluted, soil not poisoned, and the general environment cared for with affection and respect.

Only in this way will we ensure what we call a good quality of life or what the peoples of the Andes call "living well and sharing life" (*el bien-vivir y convivir*), which is the harmony of all things, first in the family, with nature, with watercourses, with the mountains, and with an economy not focused on accumulation but on subsistence.

Pope Francis exclaims: "Never have we so hurt and mistreated our Common Home as we have in the last two hundred years" (*Laudato Si'*, §53). Accordingly we must undergo "a global ecological conversion" (§5), before the process becomes irreversible. Consumption must be marked by solidarity and governed by shared moderation. As the Chinese president Xi Jinping said in 2018 in a speech to the Chinese Communist Party, "China must form a society that is moderately resourced."

Political and Social Ecology: Sustainability

Every society organizes its form of accessing natural goods and services, the way of distributing them, and how to ensure that they can reproduce and not run out. The aim is to attain sustainability, that is, to allow natural capital to meet the needs of human beings in the present and future generations and, at the same time, allow nature to rest, to regenerate, and replace what we have taken from it.

The conquest of the world and the colonization of the whole of Amerindia were carried out with extreme violence. Moreover, the Earth was not always seen in history as the Great Mother who gives us everything, but simply as an inert object, a sort of chest full of goods and services available to human beings in their project of unlimited growth.

Science and technology expanded this project, which brought great benefits for human life, from antibiotics to journeys to outer space. But at the same time it created a death machine with chemical, biological, and nuclear weapons, capable of destroying all life on Earth.

It produced two injustices. One was social: the opulent minority—less than 20 percent—of humanity were able to access 80 percent of all natural resources, and the rest, the poor 80 percent of the Earth's population, victims of injustice, had access to only 20 percent. In *Laudato Si'*, Pope Francis gives this warning: "The exploitation of the planet has already exceeded acceptable limits and we still have not solved the problem of poverty" (§27). He goes on: "These situations have caused sister earth, along with all the abandoned of our world, to cry out, pleading that we take another course. . . . [We must therefore] hear *both the cry of the earth and the cry of the poor*" (§§53, 49).

The other injustice is ecological, the destruction of entire ecosystems to the point at which the Earth is starting to show signs of distress. The Earth requires a year and a half to replace what we have taken out of it in one year.

A limited planet cannot support a project of unlimited growth. For this reason, the Earth has become unbalanced, as can be seen from global warming, climate disruption, and other extreme events. Today people say that in the past century we have inaugurated a new geological age, the Anthropocene: in other words, the human being is a hurtling meteor capable of decimating the Earth. Human beings, with their consumerist and destructive behavior, turn out to be the great threat to the future of life and the living planet, the Earth. In the words of the great biologist Edward O. Wilson, "Man has become the Satan of the Earth. . . . He has transformed the earthly paradise into a slaughterhouse."

Pope Francis takes the same line: "Doomsday predictions can no longer be met with irony or disdain. We may well be leaving to coming generations debris, desolation, and filth. The pace of consumption, waste, and environmental change has so stretched the planet's capacity that our contemporary lifestyle, unsustainable as it is, can only precipitate catastrophes" (*Laudato Si'*, §161).

This is the reason why Pope Francis insists repeatedly

that a comprehensive ecology must incorporate the question of social justice to deal with all the cries of nature and those of the mass of poor people around the world.

Mental Ecology: New Minds and New Hearts

This branch of ecology has to do with the human mind and what happens in it. Generally everything starts with some idea or a dream that takes over our mind. Today we have to change our minds.

The Earth Charter warns: "As never before in history, common destiny beckons us to seek a new beginning. . . . This requires a change of mind and heart" (Conclusion).

Changing our minds means no longer regarding the Earth as something dead, but as Gaia, a living super-organism that is self-regulating and combines physics, chemistry, and ecology to maintain life always on Earth. It is alive and our Common Home.

Changing one's heart means rescuing cordial or sensitive intelligence. We have to enrich the rational and analytic intelligence that predominates in our culture and with which we organize the world. It needs to be completed with cordial intelligence. That is where sensitivity, love, compassion, ethics, and spirituality reside.

This is what makes us feel that the pain of the world is our own, as Pope Francis emphasizes in *Laudato Si'*. He continues: "I would reiterate that 'God has joined us so closely to the world around us that we can feel the desertification of the soil almost as a physical ailment, and the extinction of a species as a painful disfigurement'" (§89). Our impulse to unite with nature cannot be genuine "if our hearts lack tenderness, compassion, and concern for our fellow human beings" (§91).

If we do not suffer with Mother Earth, how are we going to care for her as we care for our mother? Cordial reason gives rise to attitudes of respect, compassion for nature in its suffering, and love for all creatures. We call this biophilia, love for everything that lives. It is the same attitude as that of St. Francis, the patron saint of ecology, who called all creatures by the sweet name of sister and brother. Without sensitivity of heart we shall continue plundering the living Earth and its natural resources, threatening the future of life and of our civilization. Without heart, reason goes mad. Think of the Shoah, the gulags, the two world wars, the destruction of Iraq with the monuments of one of the most ancient cultures, and of the Islamic State cutting the throats of all those who would not convert to their form of Islam.

Spiritual Overall Ecology: We Are Part of the Universe

This branch of ecology, also called "deep ecology," enables us to understand our belonging to this planet Earth and also to the whole universe. We are made of the same physical and chemical elements produced millions of years ago at the heart of the great red stars. When these stars exploded, they shot these elements throughout space, giving rise to galaxies, the stars, the Sun, to our Earth, and to each one of us.

The Earth is part of the immense universe that has already been in existence for 13.7 billion years, is 28,000 light-years away from the center of our Milky Way, on the inner side of a branch of Orion's spiral.

It is a minute blue-and-white dot, lost among the billions and billions of galaxies, stars, and planets. But this is where we live, and it is from here that we think about and contemplate the grandeur of the universe in its dazzling harmony. The great English physicist and cosmologist Stephen Hawking said, in *A Brief History of Time* (1988), that if one of the four fundamental forces, gravity, which attracts all beings, were too strong, there would have been explosion after explosion, and existing creatures would not have formed. In the same way, if it had been too weak, there would not have been sufficient density for the stars to form, the Earth would not exist, and I would not be here writing about all this.

The four mysterious forces, gravity, electro-magnetism, weak nuclear force, and strong nuclear force, which always act in conjunction, are, according to the great cosmologist Brian Swimme, the way in which the ordering and intelligent spirit of the universe acts. The final detail is added by the British physicist Freeman Dyson, whom I have quoted before: "The more I examine the universe and the details of its architecture, the more I find evidence that the universe knew that one day, far in the future, we would appear."

Earth and humanity form a great, complex unity. This is what the astronauts tell us after seeing the Earth from the moon or from their spaceships. They all confirm it: "From up here there is no separation between Earth and humanity; they form a single entity." That is why we can assert that human beings are the portion of the Earth that feels, thinks, loves, and venerates. We should remember that "human" comes from the same word family as "humus," good, fertile earth. Adam, in Hebrew, comes from *adamah*, cultivable land.

This vision of totality makes us humble but at the same time proud to feel ourselves part of the universe, that being through which the universe itself has feelings, thoughts, and venerates the Originating Source of all beings. As a result, there emerges in us the feeling of reverence for that mighty and loving Force, God, who created everything and placed us on this small and beautiful planet Earth, our only Common Home.

From this primal experience there springs up in us spirituality, which is stressed so much at the end of Pope Francis's encyclical on comprehensive ecology.

> More than in ideas or concepts as such, I am interested in how such a spirituality can motivate us to a more passionate concern for the protection of our world. A commitment this lofty cannot be sustained by doctrine

alone, without a spirituality capable of inspiring us, without an "interior impulse which encourages, motivates, nourishes and gives meaning to our individual and communal activity." (*Laudato Si'*, §216)

An Ecotheology of Liberation

Comprehensive ecology and the theology of liberation have something in common. Both start with a cry of distress. Ecology starts with the cry of the Earth, of living things, of the forests, watercourses, soil and air attacked by the type of unlimited material growth promoted by the dominant worldview, especially from the cry of the Earth, a planet that has grown old and has reduced immunity.

The theology of liberation came into being through listening to the cry of distress of the economically poor, the exploited classes, humiliated cultures, Black people who are victims of discrimination, LGBTI people, and those with special needs. They are all exploited and cry out. They cry for liberation.

This concern gave rise to the various varieties of liberation theology, similarly to the varieties of ecology: sociopolitical, feminist, indigenous, Black, cultural, pastoral, general, among others. In all these varieties it is always the victim of the particular form of oppression who is the moving spirit and the protagonist of the relevant form of liberation.

It is important to remember that as long ago as the 1980s some liberation theologians realized that the same logic that exploits the oppressed and the poor classes also exploits nature and the Earth. It is well known, but worth repeating, that the trademark of liberation theology is the option for the poor, against poverty and for social justice and the liberation of the poor.

Within the category of the poor we have to include the poorest of the poor, the Earth, our Mother, the Earth that is being tortured and crucified. We have to take her down from the cross.

It was therefore not extrinsic factors that led liberation theology to incorporate the theme of ecology, but its own inner logic, which makes the poor and oppressed central.

It was also clear that it is the same industrial system, politically liberal or neoliberal in its capitalist mode of production, that produced the cry of the Earth and the cry of the poor. If we want the liberation of both, we need to move beyond this system historically. Our challenge is to offer a different cosmology and a new paradigm, friendly to the Earth and capable of liberating it from all forms of oppression.

Against the paradigm of domination we set the paradigm of essential care. Care, rather than a virtue, is a way of being, loving, not aggressive, welcoming of the other, in this case, of the Earth and the oppressed. According to the myth of care, which goes back to the Romans, as evidenced by Hyginus, the imperial librarian, which received its best philosophical description in Martin Heidegger's *Being and Time* (§§41–43), care belongs to the essence of a human being. According to the myth, care comes first. It is the ontological premise that has to exist for any being to burst into existence. Without care for all factors, no being emerges and maintains itself in existence; it fades away and dies. Equally, ethically care directs our actions in advance so that they are beneficial and not harmful.

Today more than ever, we need to cultivate the paradigm and the ethic of care, since everything, to some degree, is uncared for. Everything we love we care for; everything we care for we also love. It is care that gives origin to the culture of solidarity instead of competition, of sharing instead of individualism, of self-control and restraint instead of breaching inviolable limits, of sober consumption instead of consumerism and waste.

It is care that leads us to accompany the oppressed in their struggles and rescue the life of ecosystems, giving Mother

Earth rest and peace. Much of the biodiversity and the chemical and physical factors that sustain life are under threat (watercourses, soil, climates, micro-organisms, fibers, seeds, forests, etc.); levels of poverty are increasing dangerously around the world. Armed conflicts, in a sort of balkanization of wars, are producing increasing numbers of innocent victims and refugees, with the risk of the outbreak of an atomic conflagration (particularly in the context of the new Cold War between the United States and China), which could bring the risk of the end of the human species and of visible life on Earth. The Earth would continue, but covered with corpses.

Only the incorporation of care, as a culture and as a spirituality, can pull us out of the funeral procession of those who are heading toward their own burial. In order to achieve this, the ecotheology of liberation had to dialogue with and learn from new forms of knowledge, such as earth sciences and life sciences, quantum physics, and the new cosmology, in order to underpin its arguments. It has a special mission to contribute the values of respect, veneration, and care, inherent in the Christian faith, and fundamental values for an all-around ecology.

Finally, an ecotheology of liberation bears witness, amid the threats weighing over the future of life and Mother Earth, to the hope and the certainty that "You spare all things, for they are yours, O Lord, you who love the living" (Wis 11:26); cf. *Laudato Si'*, §§77; 89), and that God will not allow this sacred heritage, once taken up by the incarnation of the Son of God and Mary by the Holy Spirit, and entrusted to us to care for (Gen 2:15), to be totally destroyed and disappear from the face of the Earth.

The hopeful final words of the Earth Charter provide an appropriate ending to this chapter: "Let ours be a time remembered for the awakening of a new reverence for life, the firm resolve to achieve sustainability, the quickening of the struggle for justice and peace, and the joyful celebration of life" ('The Way Forward").

8

An Ethics That Is Universal and for the Common Home

There are many ethical paths based on the different cultures of humanity, from the East, from the West, and from First Peoples. The framework of Western ethics that has become globalized is based on Greek reasoning with elements from the Judeo-Christian tradition. But it is not the only one.

Today, as globalization proceeds and all cultures meet, we see, as never before in the history of thought, that the Greek word *ethos* is taking on its full meaning. For the Greeks, *ethos* meant basically the human home, not in a material sense but in its existential sense, as that portion of nature (*physis*) that we reserve for ourselves, to organize and look after in such a way that it becomes our habitat, the place where "we feel at home," protected and living in harmony with all those who live in it, with our neighbors, and the nature surrounding us.

The effort we put into caring for our home (an ethical principle) and the different ways, according to the culture, we relate within it and to the outside world in practice form what we mean by morality. Ethics and morality are like two sisters that should walk hand in hand, though this sisterly relationship doesn't always take place. *Ethos* represents universal principles, morality how these principles are put into practice in the different cultures and traditions.

However, for us today *ethos*-home is no longer our house, our city, or our country. It is all of planet Earth, which has become *ethos*-Common Home. This very fact provokes the question: What should be the common *ethos* that allows us to live together although we come from such different regions of the Earth, with our cultures, traditions, religions, and ethical values? What choices do we need to make, what coalition of values should we assemble so that human community/ society, the vast community of life, and the whole earthly community can live with a minimum of peace and justice?

What is urgently needed is to build a common basis from which we can assemble a minimum consensus that will safeguard and regenerate the Common Home, which is today under assault from ecological devastation and international social injustice, and also ensure a common future—Earth-and-humanity.

Ethics in the Planetary Phase of Humanity

Before tackling this question we need to become aware that we are living in a new stage of the history of humanity and of the Earth itself, the planetary stage. This makes it clear that we all have a common destiny and future and that we need to safeguard it because, as the situation has been changed by global warming and other ecological changes, we are all threatened. As the Earth Charter says, we must "form a global partnership to care for Earth and one another or risk the destruction of ourselves and the diversity of life" (Preamble).

This *ethos* that has to be built must take into account the basic perspective of the formation of the world as presented by the new cosmology. The Earth is the product of a long process of evolution over a period approaching 13.7 billion years. As a planet, it has existed for over four billion years. In it the elements are not just alongside each other, but inter-/retro-connected, as so strongly emphasized by the Earth Charter and Pope Francis's ecological encyclical *Laudato Si'*.

The Earth turns out to be a whole that is physical and chemical, biological, socio-anthropological, and spiritual, one and complex, which brings all these processes together to form a great living system that encourages the reproduction of life.

The vision astronauts have reported to us confirms this understanding. Their experience of contemplating the Earth from beyond the Earth and of realizing the unity of Earth and humanity is changing the state of our awareness, as it changed that of the astronauts: it becomes the awareness of people who feel interconnected with the Earth and, through it, with the whole cosmos.

Life on Earth and the life of the Earth can be seen as the result of the complexity of its history, as matter that organizes itself and, as it expands, creates itself. Human life is a subchapter of the history of life. Here there is no disjunction but conjunction; everything forms a single process that is complex (and so not linear), dynamic, and still open ahead and above.

But this is not all. With the rise of cyborgs (the combination of human beings and cybernetics), we are definitively entering a new phase of the human evolutionary process. In other words, technology is not something instrumental and external to human beings; it has been literally incorporated into human nature like a new limb. Without the resources of science and technology, we can no longer understand lived existence and human survival.

At the same time, something like a new brain is being created, a new cerebral cortex, the World Wide Web, the connection of everyone with everyone else, individual access to all the knowledge and information accumulated by humanity through the internet and the global communications network. Each person becomes, in a way, a neuron of Gaia's expanded brain.

Such a phenomenon obliges us to go beyond the modern paradigm that fractions, atomizes, and reduces. We have to adopt the contemporary holistic paradigm, which brings things into connection, relates everything to everything else, and sees the coexistence of the whole and the parts (hologram). In this way it pays proper attention to the multi-dimensionality of reality with its nonlinearity, balances and imbalances, chaos and cosmos, life and death. In the end, all things have to be contemplated in and through their eco-organizing relationship with the environment in its cosmic, natural, cultural, economic, symbolic, religious, and spiritual dimensions.

This interpretation has modified our conception of the world, of human beings and their place in the totality of beings. For new music we need new ears. Similarly, this new vision demands a new ethic, which raises the question: what sort of ethic should we live by in this new stage, which some people call the ecozoic and planetary stage?

But first I want to consider three proposals for a planetary ethic, developed from different social settings but offering significant elements for the establishment of a possible and necessary world ethics. Finally, I shall set out the one I consider most capable of being made universal: the ethics of essential and necessary care.

Religion as the Basis for a World *Ethos*

An inspiring proposal was put forward by the famous Swiss German theologian Hans Küng (1928–2021), who founded the World Ethics Foundation in Tübingen, Germany. The title of his main book on this topic makes clear his underlying thesis: *A Global Ethic for Global Politics and Economics* (1997); see also the Global Ethic Project.

In Küng's view, the aim should be not simply to construct a minimum *ethos* but first to produce a *minimum consensus* on a universally valid *ethos*. This would have to be effective and binding on all people in their different cultures. How could a consensus be constructed with such an ambitious aim?

Küng's reply was clear: through religion. The reasoning behind this view is based on the recognition that religion is the most widespread phenomenon and can form the basis for a minimum consensus among human beings. Küng insisted:

There will be no peace between nations if there is no peace between religions. There will be no peace between religions if there is no dialogue between religions. There will be no dialogue between religions unless there are global ethical standards. Our planet will not survive if there is not a world *ethos*, an ethic for the whole world.

He described this *ethos* as

the necessary minimum of common human values, fundamental rules and attitudes, or, better, it is the basic consensus about binding values, obligatory rules and basic attitudes affirmed by all religions, despite their doctrinal differences, and accepted by all people, even by those who are not religious.

In his support, Küng quoted one of the most important interpreters of the globalization process, Samuel P. Huntington, from his controversial book *The Clash of Civilizations and the Remaking of World Order* (1996):

In the modern world religion is a central force, perhaps the central force for motivating and mobilizing people. What counts for them in the end is not political ideology or economic interest. Religious convictions and family, blood and doctrine are the realities with which people identify and in function of which they fight and die.

Such an *ethos*, based on religion, has two supporting pillars, practical truth and justice as a value that cannot be abandoned to elementary ethical values shared by all religions.

Practical truth, independent of philosophical theories about truth, basically says: "We don't want to be deceived or treated as idiots anymore with regard to our social and economic situation, about the real causes of global warming, our poverty and social exclusion, about the premature deaths of our sons and daughters, about the disappearance of those close to us, about the danger that threatens us because of the undeniable ecological crisis."

Justice as a value that cannot be abandoned, as Küng emphasizes, irrespective of the erudite formulations of intellectuals, demands: "No more arrests and torture of political prisoners, no more privileges in the national and international financial system, no more exploitation of child labor, no more sexual abuse of children, no more massacres of street children, no more ethnic cleansing of entire regions." As regards this type of truth and justice there is no room for argument; what we need is worldwide convergence on values and joint actions.

To put it more formally, the minimum consensus solidifies on the right to life, on the inviolable respect for the innocent, for just treatment of prisoners, and the physical and mental integrity of every human person. It is the minimum common basis without which there can be no peaceful sharing of the planet anywhere.

It is through religion that the peoples have in practice found the way to enforce and guarantee the universal and unconditional character of this minimum consensus. Religion provides the basis for the unconditionality and the obligatory character of ethical precepts much better than abstract reasoning or rational argument, which carry little conviction and are only intelligible to some sectors of society that possess the theoretical tools that allow them to understand them.

Religion, because it is the most general (worldview), specifically the common path of the great majority of people, is more universal and intelligible. It lives by the Unconditional and seeks to bear witness to this as the deepest dimension of human life. Only the Unconditional can oblige unconditionally.

In any analysis of a situation, to ignore the religious dimension is to damage the analysis, truncate the situation, undermine the foundations of a universal ethical attitude. Only sectors of world society arrogant in their rationalism despise this type of argumentation, either because they have lost access to the experience of the sacred and religious or because they live lives alienated from the ordinary lives of their own peoples.

The core of this universal ethic is humanity, the obligation to treat human beings humanely, irrespective of their class, religion, or age. The historic religions have summed up this core in the Golden Rule: "Treat others as you would want them to treat you," or, in its negative form, "Don't treat others as you wouldn't want them to treat you."

These religions also taught "Do not kill." Translated into modern terms, this means: venerate life; develop a culture of nonviolence and respect for all life. They also taught: "Do not steal." Translated for our time, that means: act with justice and uprightness; contribute to a culture of solidarity and a just economic order. They also taught: "Do not lie." This means: speak and act with truth; commit to a culture of solidarity and a life in truth. Finally, they taught: "Do not commit adultery." I translate: love and respect each other; accept as an obligation a culture of equality and partnership between men and women.

A single world society (a geo-society) needs a single basic *ethos*; without this we cannot be sure of a common future. This time the danger is total, and rescue must also be total; there will not be a secret escape route, salvation for a privileged few. Either we are all saved, by the adoption of a world ethic, or we may all experience the fate of the great extinctions that destroyed millions of species.

Hans Küng's contribution is enormous, and among all the proposals for the world it is one of the most sensible and practical. Nevertheless, it has an internal limitation, since the majority of world societies regard themselves as secular, with secular states. Although Küng claims that it can be justified by reason, there will be difficulties in having it accepted by those who do not sign up to a religious outlook or who have chosen a different meaning for life, one that is not religious.

A World *Ethos* from the Perspective of the Poor and Their Liberation

Another proposal has been brought to us by Enrique Dussel (1934–), an Argentine theologian, philosopher, and historian currently living in Mexico (*Ethics of Liberation: In the Age of Globalization and Exclusion*, 2013).

Dussel defines his social location as being in the Global South, where the majority of suffering humanity lives. He subjects the main designers of world systems of *ethos* to a rigorous critique on the grounds that most of them are not aware of their social location, which is the center of power. From this central location it is difficult to realize that there is an underside to the world and an exclusion that are the product of closed systems, unable to include all and so permanent producers of victims.

How can they universalize their proposals if they leave out the poor and the excluded, who are the great majority of humanity? These thinkers do not make a prior ethical judgment about the historical and social system in which they are immersed and the type of reasoning they use. They take it for granted that their realities are automatically obvious and unquestionable.

From this point of view, the marginalized, and even more the excluded, are epistemologically privileged. From their position it is possible to make a critical ethical judgment on all the dominant systems of power. The excluded cry out. Their cry denounces the social and ethical system as broken and unjust because it does not include them and has to be transformed.

How can an ethical discourse be given universal reach so that it really includes everyone without distinction? Dussel is insistent that we can only attain universality if we start from partiality, from the last, from those who are left out, from the poor and oppressed, from those whose being is denied. If we start from this greater part of humanity, we will be able to open ourselves to everyone else, feeling the urgency of the necessary changes and able to ensure effective inclusion and universality. If we leave them out, we shall have selective ethical discourses, which cover things up, and are abstract and cannot be made universal.

Ethics, then, must start from the other, and not just from the other but from the other who is even more other, that is, the poor and the excluded, Black and indigenous people, oppressed women, those who are victims of discrimination for all sorts of reasons. These poor people represent more than an economic category; they represent an anthropological greatness; they have faces. The faces of the poor turn out to be unavoidable and provoking. They shout: "Help!"; stretch out their hands and beg: "I am hungry; give me something to eat."

Listening to the voice of the other, as Dussel believes, shows ethical conscience.

> Conscience is not so much applying principles to a specific case but hearing, a listening to the voice that challenges us from outside, from beyond the horizon of the system: the poor who cry for justice on the basis of their absolute, holy right, simply as a person. Ethical conscience is being able to open oneself to the other and take them seriously (responsibility), to take the side of the other against the system.

The supreme and absolute principle of ethics is: "Liberate the poor." The principle is absolute because it governs actions always, in every place and for all. "Free the poor" presupposes (a) the condemnation of a social totality, of a closed system that excludes and produces poor people; (b) an oppressor who produces poor and excluded people; (c) poor people unjustly made poor and so impoverished; (d) taking into account the mechanisms that reproduce impoverishment; (e) the ethical duty to dismantle such mechanisms; (f) the urgency to build an escape route from the system that excludes people; and, finally, (g) the obligation to bring about the new system in which all in principle have a role in participation, in justice and solidarity, including nature.

This ethics starts from the poor, but it is not just for the poor. It is for all, since no one looking at the face of an impoverished person can feel indifferent; everyone feels concerned. This ethics is fundamentally an ethics of justice, in the sense of restoring the recognition denied to the vast majority and including them in the society from which they feel—and indeed are—excluded. To achieve this, it has a hierarchy of priorities: first, to save the lives of the poor; next to ensure that all have the resources they need to live (work, housing, health care, education, security); and finally to ensure the sustainability of the Common Home, the Earth, with its ecosystems and immense biodiversity. Starting with this basic platform, we can go on to create the conditions for guaranteeing the other fundamental human rights, enshrined in so many universal declarations.

This ethics possesses an undeniably messianic character in the sense that it leads us to save lives, to wipe away tears, to arouse compassion, and encourage collaboration so that all will feel sons and daughters of the Earth and brothers and sisters of each other.

It is centered on essential things related to life and the means of life. It therefore deals directly with the impoverished majority of humankind and is an appeal to the consciences of all. It is an obvious human ethic, intelligible to and feasible for all. The intuitions it embodies will continue to apply as long as the last cry of the last oppressed person can still be heard from the farthest corner of the Earth.

This proposal, which began with Dussel, is extremely humanitarian and intelligible to all who have not yet lost the sense of the value of everyone's life, starting with those who have the least life. It originated in the Global South and is directed predominantly at the Global North, the location of the forces that produced and continue to produce the impoverishment of the majority of humankind.

The Earth Charter: The *Ethos* Centered on the Earth and Its Community of Life

A third, wide-ranging, proposal is set out in the Earth Charter: ethics centered on the Earth and humankind. It is a document that emerged from the grass roots after the 1992 Earth Summit in Rio de Janeiro, involving thousands of people from all levels of society. Some representatives of all the continents, encouraged by Mikhail Gorbachev, Steven Rockefeller, and Paulo Freire (after his death I took his place), drafted the Earth Charter from a huge quantity of material they had assembled.

This produced a document of great ethical and spiritual beauty and elegance that was officially adopted by UNESCO in 2003 to be included in educational programs throughout the world.

The Earth Charter and Pope Francis's encyclical on integral ecology, *Laudato Si'*, perhaps represent the most successful expression of the new ecological and planetary awareness in the perspective of a new cosmology and an ecozoic paradigm.

Most definitely, it starts from an integrating and holistic vision, considering the interdependencies between poverty, environmental degradation, social injustice, ethnic conflicts, peace, democracy, ethics, and the spiritual crisis. Its authors were clear: "The Earth Charter has been conceived as a declaration of fundamental ethical principles and as a practical road map with long-term significance, widely shared among all peoples. Similar to the United Nations Universal Declaration of Human Rights, the Earth Charter will be used as a universal code of conduct to guide peoples to a sustainable way of life."

The main strength of the Charter is that it defines as the central axis the category of the inter-/retro-connectivity of everything with everything else. This allows it to maintain the common destiny of the Earth and humanity and reaffirm the conviction that we form a great earthly and cosmic community.

The perspectives opened up by earth sciences, by the new cosmology, by quantum physics, by current biology, and the most solid points of the holistic paradigm of ecology are what underlie both the Earth Charter and *Laudato Si'*.

The Charter is divided into four parts: a preamble, four fundamental principles, sixteen supporting principles, and a conclusion. Running through it as a spine are the Common Home, the Earth, and the community of life.

The preamble insists emphatically that the Earth is alive and, with humankind, forms part of a vast evolving universe. It describes the threats to the Earth's dynamic equilibrium from the predatory character of the dominant development model, which has now created global warming, climate imbalances, and other extreme events.

"The protection of Earth's vitality, diversity, and beauty is a sacred trust," says the Charter's preamble. To carry out this trust, "we must decide to live with a sense of universal responsibility, identifying ourselves with the whole Earth community as well as our local communities." This must be based on "reverence for the mystery of being, gratitude for the gift of life, and humility regarding the human place in nature."

The Charter calls for "a change of mind and heart" and "a new sense of global interdependence and universal responsibility." Finally, it declares its confidence in the Earth's capacity to regenerate and in the shared responsibility of human beings to learn to love and care for the Common Home.

In its beautiful conclusion it expresses hope: "Let ours be a time remembered for the awakening of a new reverence for life, the firm resolve to achieve sustainability, the quickening of the struggle for justice and peace, and the joyful celebration of life."

To conclude this section, I venture to say that the Charter provides an outline of a world ethic that is certainly one of the most coherent, universal, and elegant that has been produced to date. Pope Francis's own ecological encyclical was inspired by it and quotes it (*Laudato Si'*, §207). If this Earth Charter is universally adopted, it will change the state of humankind's consciousness. The Earth will, finally, become central, along with all her sons and daughters who have the same origin and the same destiny as she. There will be no more room for impoverishment, unemployment, or attacks on our own Great Mother. There will be a reign of perpetual peace, as dreamed of by Immanuel Kant in his *Project for a Perpetual Peace*.

Ethos Based on Essential Care

All the proposals previously presented have their value and contribute in their own way to the construction of an *ethos* that can save the planet.

I now want to present my ideas, based on a different type of rationality, one that is cordial and sensitive, whose base is in the limbic brain, which appeared on the Earth in mammals about two hundred million years ago.

We find that in general all ethical systems, at least in the

West, give pride of place to logocentrism, modern rationalism, and anthropocentrism. Among the foundations of our
culture are the Greek *logos* and the Cartesian *cogito*.

The evolution of philosophical thought and the process
of history itself have been increasingly showing us that reason does not explain or include everything. Before reason,
something else is at work, deeper and closer to our origins,
pathos, affectivity, and essential care. Above it is intelligence,
which is the discoverer of the transcendent, the I connected
with everything and with the Mystery that underlies the
universe.

Besides this there is the a-rational and the irrational,
which show the presence of chaos alongside the cosmos, of
disorder accompanying order. *Demens* always accompanies
sapiens, the diabolic goes hand in hand with the sym-bolic.

There is a huge convergence in the admission that intelligence is permeated by sensitivity, emotions, and affections,
since these are essential characteristics of human life and
society. Michel Meffesoli talks of "sensitive reason," and the
Spanish ethics professor Adela Cortina uses the term "cordial reason."

We know that it is the heart that is the seat of the values,
the world of excellences, the affections, and the great dreams
that guide the life of ethics and spirituality.

What is the fundamental experience of human life? It is
feeling, affection, and care; it is not *logos* but *pathos*. *Sentio,
ergo sum*, "I feel, therefore I exist": this is the seminal postu-
late. *Pathos* is the ability to feel, to be affected, and to affect. It
forms the life-world, the particular and proto-primary existential set-up of a human being.

Existence is never pure existence; it is a coexistence, felt
and affected by occupation and preoccupation, by the care
and responsibility we have in the world for others, by happiness or sadness, by hope or by anguish.

The initial relation between the outside world and ourselves has no distance; it is deep active passivity: feeling the

world, others, and the I as a single complex totality. I am in the world as part of it and yet in relation to it, distinct, to see it, think about it, and shape it. Fundamentally it is a being with and not above things, a living with in a totality still without differentiation.

Martin Heidegger, in his *Being and Time*, talks about being-in-the-world as an *existential*, that is, a basic experience, constitutive of the human being, and not a mere geographical or geological accident. Accordingly, the axial structures of existence circulate around affectivity, care, eros, *pathos*, passion, com-passion, desire, tenderness, sympathy, and love. This basic feeling is not simply a movement of the psyche; it is much more, an existential quality, an essential mode of being, the way the human being is ontically structured.

Pathos is not opposed to *logos*. Feeling is also a form of knowledge, but of a different kind. It includes reason within itself, but overflows it on all sides. In the process of evolution, mammals appeared, and with them, in our planetary system, there appeared *pathos*, feeling, care, and love. Rational thought is connected to the neocortex, which emerged in the last seven million years and, in the form of *homo sapiens sapiens*, only in the last one hundred thousand years.

The person who, in a stroke of genius, saw this dimension of *pathos* was Blaise Pascal—one of the founders of probability theory, who also built a calculating machine—when he insisted that the first axioms of thought are intuited by the heart and that it is the heart that has to set the premises for any possible knowledge of reality.

David Goleman's empirical analysis, in his *Emotional Intelligence* (1995), confirmed what a particular philosophical tradition, based on Plato, Augustine, Bonaventure, Pascal, down to Freud, Heidegger, Damásio, and Meffesoli, had argued. The mind is embodied; in other words, intelligence is saturated with emotions. And it is in the emotions that the universe of existential meanings is constructed. Knowledge through pathos occurs in a process of sympathy, that is, communion with reality, suffering, and rejoicing with it and sharing its fate.

Such an understanding compensates for the vast rationalism of today's culture, dominated by instrumental and analytic reason. It is important to retrieve the rights of the heart, seat of deep feelings and values, and of cordial reason, which links it with other forms of the exercise of reason.

But the thinker who has a closely argued philosophical foundation was Martin Heidegger, whom we have already mentioned. He comments on the fable of Hyginus, the freedman of the emperor Augustus, which is about care (*Being and Time*, §§41–43). Heidegger makes clear that care is a unique way of being of men and women. Without it we cease to be human. He argues that such fundamental attributes as wanting and desiring are rooted in essential care (*Being and Time*, §41). It is only through the structure of care, he says, that they can be exercised as dimensions of being human.

Care, he says, is "an ontological constitution that always underlies everything a human being undertakes, plans and does"; "care provides in advance the ground on which all interpretation of the human being moves" (§42).

When Heidegger says "ontological constitution," he means: forms part of the essential definition of human beings and determines the structure of their activity. When he talks about care as "the ground on which all interpretation of the human being moves," he means: care is the basis for any interpretation we give of the human being. If we do not take care as the basis, we shall not be able to understand the human being as a living and active being. More simply, care—Donald Winnicott called it "concern"—functions as the prior condition for any being to become real, representing the anticipated guide of human behaviors.

If care had not been in control, as in the very first moments after the Big Bang, and the original forces released with primordial matter had not maintained a very subtle equilibrium, the conditions would not exist for dense matter—and so stars and life—to come into being, and we would not be here to talk about all this.

Care, therefore, is the prior condition for the emergence of beings. If we are not fed by it, our actions will become confused, if not irresponsible.

Care, therefore, establishes a new *ethos* and a new *morality* in the original sense of the Greek *ethos*, as I mentioned before: the way we organize our home, the world we live in with human beings and with nature.

Human beings are fundamentally beings marked by care and sensitivity, more than beings characterized by reason and will. Care is a loving relationship with reality, with the aim of ensuring its subsistence and creating space for its development, as I have explained in my investigation *Essential Care: An Ethics of Human Nature* (2008) and "Necessary Care" (2010). Care prevents future harm and regenerates what has been damaged in the past.

The equivalent concept to care in ecological language is *sustainability*, which aims to find the proper balance between the rational use of the Earth's goods and services, preserving it for us and future generations.

In everything, human beings apply and should apply care: for life, for our bodies, for our spirits, for nature, for our health, for those we love, for those who suffer, and for our homes. Without care, life perishes, since we are all sons and daughters of care. If our mothers had not taken infinite care to welcome and nurture us, we would not have been able to leave our cradles and look for our food; in a few days we would have died.

The ethic of care is clearly the most important ethical value in our time, given the degree of carelessness and negligence that hovers like a threat over the biosphere and human destiny, which has made the major world ecological organizations raise the alarm with increasing force.

So care is part of the essence of human beings; it is present in all of us and in all circumstances. This provides a common and universal basis, intelligible to all, for a planetary *ethos*. From this globalizing platform of *pathos* enriched by the tradition of the *logos*, with essential care as its main expression, are derived other dimensions of ethics, closely linked to care.

Four Principles That Sum Up Care

I want to sum up quickly the basic content of this type of ethics. I believe that four pillars support the building that is the ethics of care, in other words, four principles: (1) care in itself, (2) responsibility, (3) solidarity, and (4) compassion.

Necessary Care

We have already touched on the core of essential care. Here I want to add that the equivalent of care in ecological and political terms is *sustainability*, which aims to find the proper balance between the rational use of Earth's goods and services and its preservation for future generations. Sustainability requires us to love and care for what is invisible, those who have not yet been born, to care for every element so that it keeps the Earth, our Common Home, habitable for us and for future generations. Because life in the current world system has not taken this care, today we are suffering the harmful effects of global warming, which will affect the whole life system.

We have to move from an industrial society, extremely greedy for energy and polluting, to a society that sustains all life.

What is our initial attitude to the other? It must be one of deep respect. Each person is unique in the world, possesses value in himself or herself, and, for religious people, the other is the main revelation of the Creator. The other must be respected in his or her existence and in his or her conscience. They can never be used or debased to a means: a tool of propagation, a tool for some ideology or—worse—for some unnecessary consumer product, a means of production, a means of war, or material for scientific experimentation.

The most original cultures testify to respect for the other, whether it is living or lifeless. A Yanomami or Guaraní indigenous person performs a whole rite, asking permission from the forest to move respectfully into it or to cut down a tree in order to use its wood to make a canoe or a table.

Buddhism—which does not present itself as a religion but as a form of wisdom—teaches respect for all beings, especially those that suffer, and shows deep compassion for them. Hinduism also preaches respect and nonviolence and was embodied most convincingly in Mahatma Gandhi.

Christianity is familiar with the exemplary figure of St. Francis of Assisi, who respected all creatures, called them brothers and sisters, and treated them as such.

Here we see a different way of living in the world, alongside things, living with them and not dominating them.

The great German philosopher Arthur Schopenhauer (1788–1860), who influenced Sigmund Freud (1856–1939) and so many thinkers down to our own day, produced a whole ethical project based on respect for all creatures in the universe.

Few, however, won contemporary relevance as much as Albert Schweitzer (1875–1965), the theologian, musician, and doctor from Alsace, who abandoned a great academic and musical career in his country to serve the sufferers from Hansen's disease in Lambaréné in modern Gabon, from 1913 to his death. In Africa he produced a wide-ranging ethics of respect for every creature and life in all its forms.

The central point for Schweitzer was not Friedrich Nietzsche's will to power or Freud's desire, but the will to be and to live. Everything that exists and lives deserves to be and to live. As a result, ethics is radical respect for every creature and every life, beginning with those most threatened and suffering.

This respect does not apply merely to other human beings, but also to the whole of nature, to Mother Earth, to animals, and even to lifeless creatures. They all have the right to exist and share life with us.

Behavior like this is what is most lacking in our globalized culture: the poor are continually denied respect for their rights, members of sexual minorities are persecuted and even killed, and the dignity of the Earth is systematically violated.

A Responsibility Incumbent on All

Another attitude that we should nurture toward another person is responsibility. The other person comes to us as an offer that asks for a response. The relation between offer and response generates responsibility. We are responsible for the type of relationship we establish with the other: one of welcome and not rejection, of living together in harmony and not exclusion, of alliance (we become allies) and not enmity, of love and not hatred.

Responsibility comes into being when we become aware of the consequences of our actions for others and for nature. The imperative of the ethic of responsibility can be framed as "Act with responsibility to ensure that the consequences of your attitudes and actions are not harmful to others and not destructive of nature, life, and the Earth." Responsibility makes us see that we have the same destiny and so leads us to build a future that is good for all of us.

It is because the ethic of responsibility—that is, to respond positively to the other person in front of me—is constantly violated today that we have fundamentalism and terrorism. A fundamentalist imagines that only they possess the truth and that everything other people think or say is wrong. A terrorist is a person who is willing to destroy other people who do not think and act like them. In other words, the terrorist does not give them a responsible response and does not respect a differing opinion.

The ethic of responsibility applies especially to biotechnology, nano-technology, and to those operations that directly modify the genetic code of human beings, of other living creatures, and produce genetically modified seeds. The universe worked for 13.7 billion years, and evolution 3.8 billion, to organize the data that guarantee life and its balance. We, in one generation, want to control these very complex processes without measuring the consequences of our actions. That is why an ethic that is responsible prescribes precaution and caution as basic attitudes.

This ethic sets some tasks as priorities. For society, we have to replace the principle of competition, which uses calculating reason, with the principle of cooperation, which uses cordial reason. An especially important area of responsibility is the social and environmental responsibility of companies. They should not benefit just their owners and shareholders but should also be co-responsible for the welfare of the whole society to which they belong and in which they carry out their business activities. For the economy, it is important to move from the accumulation of wealth for a few to the production of what is sufficient and decent for all. For nature, we have to find a balance between the rational use of the goods we need and the preservation of the wealth of nature and ecology. For the spiritual atmosphere of our societies, it is important to go from the exaltation of violence, especially in the media, to a culture of peace, nonviolence, and the search for the common good.

If we play our part responsibly, even contrary winds will help to bring the ark of salvation to a safe harbor.

Universal Solidarity

Another attitude we should nurture toward others, the human home, and its inhabitants is solidarity. How should we understand solidarity?

Objectively, solidarity is part of the design of all creatures. After all, we are all interdependent on one another; we coexist in the same cosmos and in the same natural world with a common origin and a common destiny.

Living creatures, from the simplest bacterium to a human being, possess the same basic genetic code: we have the same twenty-two amino acids and the four phosphate bases. The various combinations of these elements form the Earth's immense biodiversity.

Cosmologists and quantum physicists assure us that the supreme law of the universe is that of universal solidarity and cooperation among all creatures. Even Darwin's law of natural selection, formulated with living organisms in mind, has to be thought of within this greater law of solidarity.

In addition, creatures fight not only to survive but also to realize the potential present within them. At a human level, instead of natural selection, which eliminates the weakest, we should propose care, love, and solidarity. In this way all can be included, even those who have the least chances of life.

Solidarity is present at the root of the process of hominization. Our hominid ancestors, when they went out to look for food, did not consume it as individuals but brought it back to the group and distributed it in an act of solidarity. It was solidarity that made possible the leap from animality to humanity and the creation of communities and societies, which are the expression of the human being, a social being endowed with language.

This objective solidarity must be adopted subjectively as a personal and collective project and become the lived content of social relationships. Political solidarity will either be the unifying principle of world society or there will not be a long-term future for anyone. This solidarity will have to be built from below, by the victims of social processes and those who suffer. Only then will it really include everyone.

The commandment is: "Join in solidarity with all creatures, especially human beings, because all are your companions in the planetary and cosmic adventure; join in solidarity especially with those who have been most hurt, so that all these may be included in your care and responsibility." It is also important to encourage solidarity with future generations, because they too have a right to a habitable Earth.

Our mission is to care for the creatures, to be the guardians of the common natural and cultural heritage, ensuring that the biosphere continues to be a resource for all life, and not just ours. Because of the ethic that takes responsibility, we venerate every creature and every form of life.

Compassion, the Eastern Form of Care

The human habitat (*ethos*), the other, and nature can suffer harm. There is much suffering in society and nature: millions of people suffer all sorts of need; animals such as cattle and birds in captivity are subjected to avoidable suffering; forests are cut down, land is poisoned, and watercourses are polluted. How should we behave in the face of this painful situation for which we are all, in one way or another, responsible? How can we relieve the suffering?

This is where the ethic of compassion comes in. To have compassion does not mean feeling "a bit sorry" for others, a reaction that reduces them to a condition of helplessness, as though they had no potential or strength of their own to get back on their feet. The word "compassion" itself has a positive meaning, sharing in the passion or suffering of others, suffering with them, sharing their happiness, making the journey with them.

Compassion is the principle that Buddhism left to all humankind, similar to the mercy shown by Jesus and so central to Pope Francis's messages. In the Buddhist understanding, compassion implies two attitudes, detachment from all things and care for all things. Through detachment we put a distance between ourselves and things, renouncing possession of them, and we learn to respect them in their otherness and difference. Through care we draw near to things to enter into communion with them, take responsibility for their well-being, and help them in their suffering.

This is behavior based on solidarity and love, like that of the Good Samaritan, which has nothing to do with "pity" or "charity" in the sense of remote do-gooding. Tibetan culture expresses compassion through the figure of the Buddha, with two thousand arms and two thousand eyes. With these eyes and arms he can, in his com-passion, help an unlimited number of people.

The ethic of compassion also teaches us what our relationship with nature should be like: first we should respect it in its otherness and then we should care for it. Only after that should we use it, as necessary, for our benefit.

The Rights of Mother Earth
and the Restoration of the Natural Contract

The ethical demands suggested above require us to rebuild our humanity and our civilization with a different type of relationship to the Earth, so that she can maintain her biocapacity to continue being our good and generous Mother, who gives us everything, and our Common Home.

The Natural Contract with the Earth
Has Been Broken

We urgently need to re-establish the natural contract with the Earth, since all living creatures, including ourselves, have the same basic genetic code and form the great community of life. All creatures have intrinsic value, irrespective of the use we make of them, and therefore deserve respect as endowed with dignity and rights.

Any contract is made on the basis of reciprocity, exchange, and recognition of the rights of each of the parts. Earth gives us everything, life and the means of life. In return, by virtue of the natural contract, we have the duty of gratitude, repayment, and care so that she always retains her vitality and does what she has always done for all of us.

But we have broken this contract, a long time ago. We have subjected Mother Earth to a real war, in our desperation to seize from her, without any consideration, everything we think good for our use and enjoyment. This lust has meant that in the last fifty years there has been a loss of 40 percent of forests, 50 percent of wetlands, 35 percent of mangrove swamps, 80 percent of fish stocks, and 25 percent of cultivable land. The Earth has lost significant proportions of its biodiversity (between 27,000 and 100,000 species have been wiped out annually), and global warming has done serious damage to the balance of our climate.

We can only reverse this damaging situation if we re-establish the natural contract. We must think of ourselves as the Prodigal Son in the Gospel parable and return to the Earth, our Common Home, and ask her forgiveness.

Re-establishing the Natural Contract

This forgiveness cannot be obtained by moving rhetoric but has to be reflected in a change of behavior and show the respect and care that Mother Earth deserves. She is our Mother, the Pachamama for the Andean peoples and Gaia for modern scientists. If we do not re-establish this bond of mutuality, she will find it hard to give us for nothing what she has so generously showered on us and the whole community of life for millions of years.

A point may eventually be reached at which the Earth has had enough of us. That is why sustainability is essential, to form the basis of a real re-establishment of the natural contract. Either this will happen or it is not impossible that we shall have a tragedy in the life system and the human species on a scale never known in history.

But there is something surprising. Despite the breaches of the natural contract, Mother Earth is still sending us positive signals. Despite global warming and the erosion of biodiversity, the sun still rises, the thrush still sings in the morning, the flowers smile at the passers-by, the hummingbirds still hover in front of the lilies, children are still being born and confirming to us that God still believes in humanity and that it will have a future.

Pope Francis has an encouraging message in *Laudato Si'*: "The Creator does not abandon us; he never forsakes his loving plan or repents of having created us. Humanity still has the ability to work together in building our Common Home" (§13). And he ends with this appeal: "Humanity is called to recognize the need for changes of lifestyle, production, and consumption" (§23). The Earth Charter talks about three r's: reduce, reuse, and recycle all that we use and consume.

These words sum up what we must do to re-establish the natural contract in a perspective of confidence in the Creator, who never abandons us, and in the human being's capacity for change by inaugurating a new style of relationship with nature and with Mother Earth, one of responsibility and synergy.

The Ancestral Wisdom of the First Peoples

Re-establishing the natural contract implies recovering the vision and values witnessed to by the First Peoples, well expressed in the speech attributed to Chief Seattle of the Suquamish people, delivered in the presence of Isaac Stevens, governor of Washington Territory, in 1854:

We know this: the earth does not belong to man. Man belongs to the earth. Man has not woven the net of life: he is just a thread in it. Everything he does to this net he does to himself. We would understand the intentions of the white man if we knew his dreams, if we knew what hopes he passes on to his children in the long winter nights and what visions of the future he offers their minds so that they can formulate desires for tomorrow.

The United Nations resolution of 22 April 2009 designating 22 April as International Mother Earth Day is hugely significant. Earth and ground and soil can be turned, used, bought, and sold. Earth as Mother cannot be bought or sold, but has to be loved, respected, and cared for, as we treat our own mothers. This behavior will reaffirm the natural contract, giving sustainability to our planet, because through it we will re-establish the relationship of mutuality.

Learning to Listen to Nature

Another lesson the First Peoples teach us is how to listen to nature. Our whole culture, so influenced by ancient Greece, is based on seeing. It is no accident that the central category, the idea (*eidos* in Greek), has to do with vision. Tele*vision* is its supreme example. We have developed our vision to an amazing degree. With immensely powerful telescopes we penetrate the depths of the universe to see the most distant galaxies, and we also have sophisticated equipment that allows us to see the traces of the latest elementary particles and the intimate mystery of life. Seeing is everything for us, but we have to realize that this is the mode of being of the Western human being, but not of all.

Listening is a different sort of relationship with nature. The cultures close to us in South America, such as those of the Andes (the Quechua, Aymara, and others) are structured around listening. Logically, they also see, but their distinctive feature is listening to the messages of what they say. The farmer from the Bolivian *altiplano* says: "I listen to nature. I know what the mountain is saying to me." A shaman testifies: "I listen to the Pachamama and know what message she is giving me."

Everything speaks: the sun, the moon, the lofty mountains, the peaceful lakes, the deep valleys, the fleeting clouds, the lush forests, the brightly colored birds, and the wild animals. People learn to listen carefully to these voices. Books are not important for the First Peoples because they are dumb, while nature is full of voices. They have become so specialized in this way of listening that they know, when they see the clouds, when they listen to the winds, when they watch the llamas or the movement of the ants, what will happen in nature. This reminds me of an ancient theological tradition originating with St. Augustine and systematized by St. Bonaventure in the Middle Ages: the first divine revelation is the voice of nature, God's real speaking book. But, because we lost the ability to hear, God in his mercy gave us a second book, the Bible, so that by listening to its contents we could once more hear what nature is saying to us.

A tragic example of what listening and not reading means is what Francisco Pizarro did in 1532 in Cajamarca. In a treacherous ambush he captured and imprisoned the Inca emperor Atahualpa, and ordered the Dominican friar Vicente Valverde, with the help of his interpreter, Felipillo, to read him the "demand," a terrible text in Latin that required the indigenous to accept baptism and submit to the Spanish monarchs, because the pope, God's representative, had so ordered. If they refused, they could be enslaved for disobedience.

The emperor asked him what was the source of this authority. Valverde handed him a Bible. Atahualpa took it and held it to his ear. Having heard nothing, he threw the

Bible on to the ground. It was the signal for Pizarro to order the massacre of the whole royal guard and imprison the Inca emperor. As we see, listening was everything for Atahualpa. The book of the Bible said nothing to him.

For Andean culture, everything is structured within a web of living relationships that carry meaning and messages. They perceive the thread that runs through everything, unifies it, and gives it meaning. We Westerners see the trees, but not the wood.

For us things are isolated from each other. They are dumb. The only talking is ours, and it is so loud that it drowns the words of nature. We take things out of the context of their relationships, which is why our language is formal and cold. In it we constructed our philosophies, theologies, doctrines, and dogmas. But that is our way of perceiving the world and not that of all peoples. We do not have the right to impose it on them, as we did in the colonial process of evangelization. The peoples of the Andes help us to relativize our claim to universality. We can express our messages in different ways that are inclusive and seek a relationship, and not in those we are accustomed to use, supposedly objective, but silent. The people of the Andes challenge us to listen to the messages that come to us from all sides.

These days we have to listen to the warnings that come to us from the black clouds, the wild waves of the sea, the forests on hillsides, the rivers that burst their banks, the gulfs that suddenly open up, the falling rocks. The sciences of nature help us in this task of listening, but it is not our cultural habit to pick up warnings from what we see. Our deafness thus makes us victims to terrible disasters, such as the landslides that occurred in the mountain region of the state of Rio de Janeiro in 2011, killing nearly nine hundred people. The landslides buried a whole valley and part of a city.

We only dominate nature if we obey it, that is, listen to what it teaches us. Deafness leaves us with bitter lessons.

The Rights of Mother Earth

The former president of Bolivia, the Aymara indigenous Evo Morales Ayma, has often said that the twenty-first century will be the century of the rights of Mother Earth, of nature, and of all living creatures. In his address to the United Nations General Assembly on 22 April 2009, which I attended, and where I presented the theoretical justification for calling the Earth Mother, Morales listed some of these rights of Mother Earth:

- the right of the Earth and its biocapacity to regenerate
- the right to life, guaranteed to all living creatures, especially species threatened with extinction
- the right to a clean life: Mother Earth has the right to live free from any sort of contamination and pollution
- the right to live well, guaranteed to all citizens
- the right to harmony and balance with and among all and everything
- the right to a connection with Mother Earth and with the whole of which we are a part

This vision allows us to renew the natural contract with the Earth, which, acting in conjunction with the social contract between citizens, will in the end reinforce planetary sustainability. For the First Peoples such an attitude was natural. We, to the extent that we have lost the connection with nature, have also lost the awareness of our relationship of recognition and gratitude to her. Hence the importance of revisiting them and learning from them the respect and veneration to which the Earth has a right.

Mother Earth: Subjectivity and Dignity

When we claim—with the support of much of the scientific community—that the Earth is a living complex Super Being, with a myriad of living creatures that make up the biosphere, logically we are admitting that she, like other animate creatures, and with much more right than they, possesses subjectivity and dignity and therefore enjoys rights. These rights imply duties on our part.

To say that the Earth has subjectivity, dignity, and rights implies that she has, as regards subjectivity, a history. In some real but mysterious way, she has an ability to feel, to have intentionality, to be governed by an inner rational order, in short to be spiritual. We human beings are the Earth that feels, thinks, and loves; together with her we perform all these operations.

Is the Universe Conscious?

I said earlier that spirit is just as ancient as matter. It has existed from the moment that the first relationships were established between the primordial particles. Accordingly, first it was in the universe. The universe itself, as maintained by the great mathematician and quantum physicist Amit Goswami (*The Self-Aware Universe*, 1993), is inhabited by spirit. Because it is first in the universe, it is also on the Earth, part of this universe and, naturally, also in us.

So we can say that the universe itself, of which the Earth is a part, shows itself to be conscious through the conscious Earth; through it, it contemplates itself and becomes aware of its majesty and beauty.

This subjectivity has a history; that is, it is within the immense cosmogenic process in which everything is interlinked, exchanging information and so becoming enriched, to the point at which, at a moment of extreme complexity, the consciousness that was hidden in all things emerged and became self-aware in human beings, men and women.

That moment represents the emergence of what we are, the conscious portion of the Earth, which in its turn is the conscious portion of the universe. Now, this human being is the Earth itself that feels, thinks, loves, cares, and venerates. One of the greatest moral achievements of history was to recognize the human dignity that is expressed in basic and inalienable rights. These human rights, because we are the thinking Earth, should also be attributed to her. Modern thinkers have called her Gaia, the Greek deity that represents the vitality and biocapacity of the Earth, truly Mother because she brings into being all the living creatures that exist on her soil, in the rivers, seas, and oceans.

The Twenty-First Century: The Century of the Rights of Mother Earth

The most striking claim in the speech by Bolivian president Evo Morales Ayma in the UN General Assembly on 22 April 2009, when 22 April was declared International Mother Earth Day, was perhaps the following:

> The past century, the twentieth, was the century of human rights. In the twentieth century, civil and political rights were recognized from 1948 on. In 1966, economic, social, and cultural rights were recognized. . . . The twenty-first century is the century of the rights of Mother Earth and of all living beings. If we are to live in harmony with nature, we need to recognize that not only we human beings have rights but that the planet does as well. Animals, plants, and all living beings have rights that we must respect.

Here we meet the new cosmology and the new paradigm, centered on the Earth and life. We are no longer in the anthropocentrism exacerbated by the ideas of the modern era, which ignored the intrinsic value of every creature, irrespective of what it could be used for. There is a steadily growing awareness that all that exists deserves to exist and that everything that lives deserves to live. And it is up to us to welcome their existence, defend it, and ensure that they have the conditions to continue evolving.

Consequently, we must enrich our concept of democracy to make it a biocracy or a socio-ecological democracy, because all the elements of nature, at their own levels, make up human sociability. Would our cities still be human without plants, animals, birds, rivers, and clean air?

Today we know from the new cosmology that all creatures have not only mass and energy but are also conveyors of information, have levels of subjectivity and history as a product of the relationships they maintain among themselves, which mark them. This is the scientific basis that justifies the broadening of the concept of legal personality to all creatures, especially living creatures.

Michel Serres, the French philosopher of science, rightly remarked: "The Declaration of the Rights of Man rightly said that 'all men have rights,' but wrongly thought that 'only men have rights.'" It took a long battle—and it is still not finished—for the rights of women to be fully recognized, or those of indigenous people and Black people. Today much hard work is required to secure the recognition of the rights of nature, ecosystems, and Mother Earth.

Just as we invented citizenship, Jorge Viana's government of the Brazilian state of Acre coined the expression "forest-ship," by which it meant the way to live in harmony with the Amazon rain forest and with all the creatures, goods, and services it provides.

President Morales asked the United Nations to produce a charter of the rights of Mother Earth and suggested the main elements, which I mentioned earlier.

This shows us how far we are from the capitalist conception that held us hostage for centuries, and still holds us, according to which the Earth is seen as a mere means of production, without purpose, a reserve of resources we can exploit for our comfort and enrichment. We lacked the sense that the Earth is really our Mother. And a mother should be respected, venerated, and loved. This was stressed by the president of the UN General Assembly session of 21 April 2009, the Nicaraguan Miguel d'Escoto Brockmann, when he closed the session: "Mother Earth, after all, nurtures and sustains life and our very humanity. It is only right that we, as sisters and brothers all, take care of Mother Earth in return." Accordingly he appealed to everyone to listen carefully to the indigenous peoples and small farmers since, despite all the pressures against them, they keep alive the connection with nature and Mother Earth, producing in harmony with her rhythms and with the support available from each ecosystem, in contrast to the rapacity of agrobusiness, which acts without respecting the cycles and rhythms of nature and Mother Earth.

The decision to accept that there should be an International Mother Earth Day, always on 22 April, is more than a symbol. It is an about-face in our relationship with the Earth; it represents a new state of consciousness and belonging to nature and Mother Earth, breaking with the dominant model, which uses violence against her, plunders her, and treats her without any respect, forgetting that she is the source from which we receive life and all the marvelous benefits of creation.

Will Human Beings Disappear from the Face of the Earth?

We have already looked at the damage human beings have done in their own home, the Earth, especially in recent centuries, characterized by the growth of industry and the introduction of technology into all our relationships with nature, seeking progress understood as the unlimited increase in material goods (cars, domestic appliances, trains, airplanes, and so many other conveniences of everyday life).

We have also learned that the Earth is not, as many people imagine, a warehouse filled with supplies that can be sold and used, but a living Being, complex and unique. It has been called Gaia, the ancient Greek name for the living Earth, similar to the Andean Pachamama.

And in recent times we have been taken aback by an unprecedented and alarming fact: we are beginning to feel in practice the limits of the Earth, the fact that it is over-loaded and its elements basic for life are being exhausted day by day. One way of illustrating this is the calculation of Earth Overshoot Day, that is, the date when humanity's demand for ecological resources and services in a given year exceeds what Earth can regenerate in that year. The date for 2020 was 22 August. From that date every year, in order to maintain the level of consumption of the powerful—to which we have become accustomed—we have to tear what we want violently from Earth's reserves.

Earth, like all living things, can get sick. Even so, she pos-sesses great capacity for regeneration. Nevertheless there are limits than cannot be breached, and we have breached them. The human species gave Earth many injuries and diseases, and this can be seen in many ways, especially in the changes to the climate and transformations that are easily visible.

The majority of people, however, do not see the connec-tion between these transformations (tsunamis, hurricanes, floods, prolonged droughts, etc.) and global warming. They think that one is not related to the other and so create a soci-ety of blind people, as in José Saramago's novel *Blindness*, without noticing that they are approaching an abyss.

If we do not reduce the greenhouse gases that cause warming and damage the biosphere, we may experience phenomena of mass destruction, as occurred in the great extinctions. If as early as this century we have a temperature increase of $4°-6°C$, much of the Earth's biotic capital may disappear, as in the Cambrian period, 570 million years ago, when 80 to 90 percent of living species simply disappeared.

Do we want this for ourselves? We are creating the con-ditions that may lead us inevitably to a tragic end. Never in human history has there been a similar threat; we may just disappear. I would say more: we have played so fast and loose with Gaia that suddenly she may decide that she no longer wants us on her face.

We are too aggressive and destructive, to the point of introducing the principle of self-destruction (Carl Sagan). We are threatening ourselves with destruction by nuclear, chemical, and biological weapons. We are a permanent danger to other creatures; and, finally, as the French philosopher of ecology Michel Serres alleged in his book *World War* (Paris, 2008), we have devised a strategy of total war against the Earth and attacked it on all fronts.

According to the winner of the 1995 Nobel Prize for Chemistry, the Dutchman Paul J. Crutzen, we have created a new geological era, the Anthropocene, in which human beings are the great threat to the biosphere.

One thing, however, is undeniable: we have no chance at all of winning this war against Earth. Earth is more resistant and stronger than we are; she can destroy us. We may tragically see the Earth covered with corpses, but she will continue on her course for millennia to come, traveling within the solar system.

It is in such a context that the question whether human beings might disappear from the face of the Earth becomes unavoidable. Unfortunately we have to say: yes, it is not impossible. The only hope we are left with is that it is a possibility, and even a probability, if we leave ecological conditions as they are. But there is also the possibility that, when the danger is at its greatest, we will invent strategies to save us. As the German poet Friedrich Hölderlin said, "But where the danger is, also grows the saving power."

We should listen to some voices of great scientific seriousness, known for their wisdom, because they have many warnings for us and call us to collective responsibility. Among the many, I have selected some of the most notable.

The first is a winner of the Nobel Prize for Chemistry, Christian de Duve, from Belgium, who wrote in his famous book *Vital Dust* (1995): "Biological evolution is on a runaway course toward severe instability. In a way, our time recalls one of those major breaks in evolution signaled by mass extinctions" (p. 271). Previously it was hurtling meteors that threatened the Earth; today the hurtling meteor is called *homo sapiens et demens*, doubly demented.

Théodore Monod (1902–2000), perhaps the last great naturalist, left as his testament a questioning text, "And if the human adventure were to fail?" (*Et si l'aventure humaine devait echouer* [Paris: B. Grasset, 2000]). In it he insists: "We are capable of wild and mad conduct; from this point on we may fear anything, anything at all, even the annihilation of the human race" (p. 246). And he adds: "It would be the just reward for all our acts of madness and cruelty" (p. 248).

The U.S. biologist E. O. Wilson, who coined the word "biodiversity," argues in his exciting book *The Future of Life* (New York: Knopf, 2003): "Humanity has so far played the role of planetary killer. . . . The conservation ethic, whether expressed as taboo, totemism or science, has generally arrived too late and too little to save the most vulnerable of life forms. . . . Perhaps we will act in time" (p. 102). In another of his books, *The Creation: An Appeal to Save Life on Earth* (New York: Norton, 2006), he suggests a sacred alliance between religion and science; for him these are the two forces that most mobilize humankind to avoid the annihilation of life. If this alliance does not take place, we run the risk of disappearing.

We cannot disregard the opinion of James Lovelock, who advanced the "Gaia hypothesis" in his two books, whose titles say it all: *The Revenge of Gaia* (New York: Basic Books, 2006) and *The Vanishing Face of Gaia* (New Westminster, BC: Post Hypnotic Books, 2011). In an interview with the Brazilian magazine *Veja* in 2006, Lovelock confirmed his warnings and related them to the Brazilian ecological situation. He was dramatic: "By the end of the century, 80 percent of the human population will disappear. The remaining 20 percent will live in the Arctic and on a few other continents where temperatures are lower and there is a bit of rain. Almost the whole of Brazil will be too hot and dry to live in." This forecast was confirmed by a 2013 report from the Intergovernmental Panel on Climate Change (IPCC), and the final document mentioned Brazil and its Amazon region: it concluded that we would have a hot summer throughout the year.

Another extremely authoritative voice is that of the United Kingdom's Astronomer Royal, Sir Martin Rees. In 2003 he published a categorical book, *Our Final Hour: A Scientist's Warning: How Terror, Error, and Environmental Disaster Threaten Humankind's Future in This Century—On Earth and Beyond* (New York: Basic Books). He showed how nanotechnology, genetic engineering, and biogenetics, disguised as scientific progress, can produce toxic elements, bacteria and viruses that will escape control and threaten the physical and chemical basis of life and the very future of life and our species on the planet. Rees believes that we are on an extremely dangerous course, even in the last stage, with no time to pull back.

To avoid such a catastrophe of apocalyptic dimensions we need a common sense of collective responsibility as regards our future as the human species. We also need much wisdom to make the right decisions, since this time no mistakes are allowed.

All the signs are that we are running out of time. Albert Jacquard, the famous French geneticist, implied this in the title of one of his last books, *Has the Countdown Already Started?* (2009). Possibly we are too late, as it seems we have passed the point of no return.

My hope lies in a different direction. As evolution is not linear and has frequent breaks or quantum leaps up as a result of greater complexity, and as there is the indeterminate and floating character of all energies and all matter, described in the model of quantum physics developed by Werner Heisenberg and Niels Bohr, we cannot rule out the emergence of another level of consciousness that awakens humankind to the threat of its extinction, so that it organizes all the scientific and social resources that could save the biosphere and planet Earth.

The sum of the energies of all the movements and groups that want the other world that is possible and necessary has brought about an immeasurable morphogenetic wave that would involve everyone and force a quality leap. That is how we would be saved, though, it is true, not without having to pay a heavy price for this leap: the dismantling of this type of world that is hostile to life for it to be replaced by a biocentered world, a true "land of good hope," as Ignacy Sachs and Ladislau Dowbor have called it.

If this does not happen, the disappearance of our species would mean an unprecedented disaster for our universe, for the history of life and for the history of human life (see Paul Collins, *Judgment Day: The Struggle for Life on Earth* [Maryknoll, NY: Orbis Books, 2011]). It would be a regression like those at the dawn of the planet's history.

Nevertheless, we must consider the following idea, fruit of the very dynamic of cosmogenesis and biogenesis: assuming that human beings as a species disappear, even so the principle of intelligibility and amorization would be preserved. It is present first in the universe and only subsequently in us human beings.

This principle is as ancestral as the universe. It comes from the very first moments after the great explosion, when the Higgs field was formed and the first elementary particles, such as the quarks and protons, started to interact. They brought into being networks of relations and units of information and complex orders. This was the first sign of what was later to be called spirit, that capacity to create units and patterns of order and ultimate meaning. If the human species disappeared, spirit would emerge, one day, perhaps after millions of years of evolution, in some being more complex and better than the present one.

Who Would Be the Human Being's Successor?

Théodore Monod even suggests a possible successor to us, already present in current evolution, the cephalopods, which belong to the mollusc species, like octopus and squids. Some of them have a remarkable anatomical refinement: their heads have a cartilaginous capsule that functions as a skull, and they have eyes like vertebrates. They also possess a highly developed mental system, including a double memory, whereas we have only one (*Et si l'aventure humaine devait echouer*, pp. 247–48).

Without ignoring the risks I have mentioned, I am optimistic: we will get sensible and learn to be wise and to prolong the human project, purified by the great crisis that will refine us. But it is important here and now to show love for life (what Wilson calls biophilia) in its majestic diversity, have com-passion for all who suffer, bring about rapidly the necessary social justice and the urgent ecological justice, which means respecting and loving every creature, particularly the Great Mother, the Earth. We are urged to this by the Judeo-Christian scriptures: "Choose life so that you and your descendants may live" (Deut 30:19); and God presented himself as a passionate lover of life: "You love all things that exist" (Wis 11:24). Let's move fast. There's no time to waste.

Finally, there is a short reflection that is theological in nature, since theology has the task of dealing with the last ends of human beings and the universe (eschatology). First of all, we have to recognize that we are mortal since this was God's will. One day we shall reach our climax and disappear; this happens naturally to hundreds and thousands of living organisms day after day. After millions of years of evolution it will be our turn to give way to other creatures emerging on the Earth. Even the Earth herself may be burned to a cinder as a result of the extreme heat produced by the burning of the Sun's helium, after all the oxygen has been consumed.

I would say briefly: if human beings fail in their planetary adventure, it will of course be an enormous tragedy. But it would not be an absolute tragedy. Human beings have already one day perpetrated this. When the Son of God took on our humanity, we murdered him by nailing him to a cross. Only then did original sin take shape; it is a historical process of the gradual denial of life. It is perverse to kill a creature, but a greater perversity to kill the Creator who became human.

To secure some light we can think of these issues in terms of quantum physics and the new cosmology. Evolution is not linear; it accumulates energy and takes leaps. This is what is also suggested to us by the vision outlined by Niels Bohr and Werner Heisenberg: hidden virtualities coming from the Quantic Vacuum, from that indecipherable Ocean of Basic Energy, the Abyss that generates all creatures and underlies and pervades the universe, can break in and change the direction of evolution.

I find it hard to accept that our destiny, after millions of years of evolution, should have such a miserable end in the next few generations. There will be a quantum leap—this is our faith and hope—possibly in the direction that Pierre Teilhard de Chardin suggested back in 1933: the bursting in of the noosphere, that is, that state of consciousness and relationship with nature and among human beings that will bring about a new convergence of minds and hearts. This would create a new level of human nature and of Earth's history.

Then we would have the confirmation of the remark of Ernst Bloch, who defined the "principle of hope": "The real genesis is not at the beginning, but at the end." Human beings, nature, and the universe have just been born.

In this perspective the current scene would not be a tragedy but a crisis, which refines, purifies, and brings things to maturity. It announces a new beginning, labor pains full of promise and not the agony of someone about to die or the aborting of the human adventure. We shall still spread our light.

What is important to recognize is that the world as such is not coming to an end, but possibly this type of senseless world that loves war and devastates nature. We shall inaugurate a human world that loves life, strips violence of its mystique, has care and reverence for all creatures, brings about true justice, social and ecological, which, finally, allows us to be on the Mount of the Beatitudes and not in the vale of tears.

Or, finally, we shall have learned to treat all human beings in a human way, and all other creatures with respect and compassion. This possibility is among the possibilities hidden in our human condition, in nature and in the universe, for through us the universe thinks itself, the Earth achieves its consciousness, and we become the priests who celebrate the grandeur of creation, called to enjoy the happiness of existing and living within a process that has lasted billions of years, of which we are the heirs and representatives.

We have to implore Mother Earth with all our strength to forgive us and not to condemn us to disappear. In terms of cosmic time, we have existed only for a few minutes. We are still being made and still growing, and we have not learned properly what our place is among all other creatures or our true mission in the inheritance we have received from the universe. We are still learning. More and more, the awareness is growing that we were created creators to complete the work that is under way and with the specific ethical and spiritual mission to care for the Garden of Eden and protect all the riches that flourish there. That garden is Mother Earth, and we are her guardians and caregivers.

9

Spirituality, the Depths of a Human Being

At dramatic moments of history, whether individual or collective, human beings plunge into the deepest levels of themselves and ask radical questions. What am I doing in this world? What is my place among all other creatures? What should I do to ensure that this world offers hope for all and for our Common Home? What can I hope for after this life?

What Makes People Seek Spirituality?

It is in this context that we have to place the question of spirituality. It emerges as one of the primary sources, though not the only one, of new inspiration, of hope for good news, of a hopeful outlook and capacity for self-transcendence. After all, human beings feel fully human only when they are trying to be superhuman. The reason is that their experience is that they are an infinite project, as I have insisted many times.

Everyone is talking about spirituality. It is a constant theme in our contemporary culture, not only in the sphere of religion, which is its natural place, but also in the sphere of human searching, both among young people and among intellectuals, famous scientists, and, to my surprise, among high-ranking business leaders, moving in the centers of economic power both nationally and internationally, executives of multinationals and other power brokers. They want to talk about issues such as social changes, the new model of civilization, the productivity of new technology and artificial intelligence, and the urgent need for a human spirituality.

It used to be rare in the dominant culture for business leaders to be concerned with spirituality or questions to do with the meaning of life or the meaning of the universe. But times have changed, and business leaders with them. This fact shows the scale of the crisis that is devastating us. It means that the material goods promoted by marketing, and the productivist arguments that push them, the world of values that inspires their activities, the savage competition with no spirit of cooperation, must not be enough. There is a deep void, a huge hole in their existence, raising issues such as gratuitousness and spirituality, the future of life and of the Earth system. This existential hole is the size of God, and so only God can fill it.

But it is important always to keep alive our critical spirit because spirituality can also be used to make money. There are real businesses that use talk of spirituality to create an army of followers. These religious leaders often talk more to the pockets of their listeners than to their hearts.

But we should never forget that the people endowed with a permanent spirituality are people regarded as ordinary, who live upright lives with a sense of solidarity and cultivate the sacred space of the Spirit, whether in their religions and churches or in the way they think, act, and interpret life.

What is important, however, is that throughout the world there is a demand for nonmaterial values, for a redefinition of human beings as creatures that are looking for a more fulfilling meaning than the accumulation of material consumer goods, and are looking for intangible values that light up and give meaning to life.

Everywhere we find human beings angry at the future prescribed for them in advance in terms of the political culture in which we are obliged to live, who refuse to accept the paths that humankind is being forced to follow, of production for its own sake, consumption, and waste. They are saying: "We deserve a better future. We need to drink from different wells. We need a light that shows us the right way and shows us an encouraging picture of our common future."

So What Is Spirituality Really?

Now we have to ask the question directly: What is spirituality after all? Once the Dalai Lama was asked the question and he gave an extremely simple answer:

Spirituality is what brings about an inner change in a human being.

Because the questioners weren't sure what he meant they asked him the question again:

But if I practice religion and keep the traditions, isn't that spirituality?

The Dalai Lama answered:

It might be spirituality, but unless it brings about a transformation in you, it isn't spirituality.

And he added:

A blanket that no longer keeps you warm stops being a blanket.

The person who had asked the question interrupted:

Does spirituality change or is it always the same?

And the Dalai Lama said:

As the ancients used to say, times change and people change with them. What was spirituality yesterday doesn't need to be spirituality today. What people generally call spirituality is just the memory of old religious ways and methods.

And he ended:

The cloak must be cut to fit the person, and not the people cut to fit the cloak.

The main thing we should remember from this short dialogue with the Dalai Lama is that spirituality is what produces a change in us. Human beings are always changing because they are never finished; they are always completing themselves, physically, socially, and culturally. But there are changes and changes. There are changes that do not transform the basic structure; they are superficial and external or merely decorative.

But there are changes that are internal; they are real alchemical transformations, able to give a new meaning to life or open up new areas of experience and depth that lead to the heart itself and the Mystery of all things. Quite often such changes occur in the sphere of religion, but not always. Today the unique feature of our time is that spirituality is being discovered as a dimension of human depth, as the point for the full opening up of our individuality and a space of peace in the middle of social and existential conflicts and desolation.

The Distinction between Spirituality and Religion and Their Relationship

It is therefore important, from the start, to introduce a distinction, not a separation, between religion and spirituality. In fact, the Dalai Lama himself has made this distinction brilliantly in his book *Ancient Wisdom, Modern World: Ethics for the New Millennium* (1999), an international bestseller. In this book he deals clearly with issues relating to ethics, religion, and spirituality. Allow me to quote an illuminating extract:

> Religion I take to be concerned with belief in the claims to salvation of one faith tradition or another—an aspect of which is acceptance of some form of metaphysical

or supernatural reality, including perhaps an idea of heaven or *nirvana*. Connected with this are religious teachings or dogma, rituals, prayer and so on. Spirituality I take to be concerned with those qualities of the human spirit—such as love and compassion, patience, tolerance, forgiveness, contentment, a sense of responsibility, a sense of harmony—which bring happiness to both self and others. Whilst ritual and prayer, along with the questions of *nirvana* and salvation, are directly connected with religious faith, these inner qualities need not be, however. There is thus no reason why the individual should not develop them, even to a high degree, without recourse to any religious or metaphysical belief system. (p. 23)

As we see, these reflections are crystal-clear and show the distinction that has to be made between religion and spirituality. Once they are distinguished, they can relate and coexist, but without necessarily depending on each other.

The Dalai Lama is one of those persons with messianic characteristics, since it is the role of the messiah to console, wipe away tears, give hope, and bring peace. Few people have such a gift as the Dalai Lama and Pope Francis for consoling the afflicted, giving the despairing a meaning, and preaching peace as the result of dialogue between religions, like an embrace between peoples in the perspective of saving humankind as a family and ensure a future for our Common Home, planet Earth. They travel the world preaching this gospel.

Once in Berlin I heard the Dalai Lama give this testimony:

I think that we Tibetans who live in exile in India, having lost our homeland, are following the same vocation as the Jews when they lost their land and were deported to exile in Babylon. It was a favorable opportunity to unite traditions and write the sacred scriptures, spreading monotheism among the peoples, that is, the belief in one God, who must be the God of all peoples.

And he went on:

> Perhaps the spiritual meaning of our exile is that it forces us to travel the world to talk about spirituality, about peace among the peoples, about dialogue between religions. This is what I am doing, with deep commitment and great humility.

I believe that the Dalai Lama and Pope Francis, more than other spiritual leaders, are carrying out this mission with great seriousness, and great good humor, and at the same time with a language that comes from the depths of their hearts and is therefore deeply true, moving, and convincing,

So we have to insist that without religion we cannot recover the crucial relevance of spirituality for our time, marked as it is by the secular vision of the world and by the rediscovery of the mysterious complexity of human subjectivity.

In this context the moving testimony of one of the world's most beloved writers is relevant, that of Antoine de Saint Exupéry (1900–1944), the author of *The Little Prince*. From his words we can deduce that an ethics of Earth is not enough; we need to accompany it with spirituality. This has its roots in cordial and sensitive reason, and it is from there that we are led to cultivate the spirit, to be passionate about caring, and to have a serious commitment to love, responsibility, and compassion for our Common Home.

In a posthumous text, written in 1943, before his plane plunged into the Mediterranean, Saint-Exupéry said: "*Letter to General X* says with great emphasis: 'There is only one problem, only one, to rediscover that there is a life of the spirit, even higher than the life of intelligence, the only life that satisfies a human being.'"

In another text—written in 1936, when he was a correspondent for *Paris Soir* during the Spanish Civil War—entitled "We Have to Give Life Meaning," he returns to the theme of the life of the spirit: "we need to understand each other. A human being cannot be fully realized except alongside other human beings, through love and friendship; however, human beings are not united simply by coming close to each other, but by merging with their own divinity. In a world that has become a desert, we are thirsty, thirsty to find comrades in those with whom we share our bread." He ends *Letter to General X* by saying, with reference to his fellow aviators: "They have so much need of a God!"

And it is true; only the life of the spirit fully satisfies a human being. It represents a beautiful synonym for spirituality, which is not infrequently identified or confused with religious feeling. The life of the spirit is more; it is a primordial element of our deep dimension, an anthropological element like intelligence, will, or libido, something that is part of our essence.

We know how to take care of the life of the body, which these days is a real religion practiced in so many gyms. Psychoanalysts of various schools help us to look after the life of the psyche, how to keep our impulses in balance, pacify the angels and demons that inhabit us in order to live a relatively balanced life.

But in our culture we practically forget to cultivate the life of the spirit, which is our most radical dimension, where we house the big questions, where the most daring dreams nest and the most generous utopias are developed. The life of the spirit is nourished by nontangible goods such as love, friendship, companionship, care, and openness to the infinite. Without the life of the spirit we wander around, rootless and without a meaning to guide us and give life a savor.

An ethic of the Earth will not survive for long alone, without this additional lift that is given by the life of the spirit. It summons us to rise, to actions that will save and regenerate Mother Earth.

Saint-Exupéry's words have special value because they come not from some theologian or adherent of a church or religion but from a pilot with a passion for human beings, about whom he meditated so much in his little plane on long, dangerous flights.

Even if it sometimes obscures spirituality, religion will never lose its value, above all because it promises salvation to human beings, defends the lives especially of the most vulnerable, and opens to us the dimension of eternity. It shows the way to reach that eternity, the ethical and spiritual path. In this way all religions provide a vision of God, of the world to come, about what human beings are and what they ought to do in this world. They formulate doctrines and indicate paths to the light.

But religions do not just deliver sermons; they also emphasize practices. Religions are sources of ethics, that is, codes of good behavior. In the case of Christianity it is the behavior that really saves—not the sermons but the practice. Buddhism preaches the same message.

In his book on ethics that we mentioned earlier, the Dalai Lama often says that religions only save by making possible entry into nirvana and the transfiguration of people if they are able to transform the vision of the world into a completely coherent practice, in a feeling of love for others, compassion for those who suffer, a sense of responsibility for the lives of our fellows and a life of total dispossession that leaves open to welcoming everything reality confronts us with.

If we are able to develop this practice, we shall be able to create a path that leads inexorably to what is the happiness of the world to come or nirvana, the supreme fulfillment of the human being. In the Dalai Lama's own words, "The aim of spiritual and, in the widest sense, ethical practice, is . . . to transform and perfect the individual's *kun-long* [which he says means roughly 'disposition' or 'mind-state'] to make us better human beings" (*Ancient Wisdom*, p. 33).

Religion: An Obstacle to Spirituality?

Religions represent one of human beings' most excellent constructions. All of them work with the divine, the sacred, with the spiritual, but they do not hold the monopoly on the spiritual. The spiritual is an anthropological fact, part of the dimension of depth.

It is true that religions can become ends in themselves and assert their autonomy, allying religious powers with other ideological and political powers for interests that are not always clear. For centuries there was an alliance between throne and altar, but under the control of the altar. With the exception of the two world wars, the wars of religion were perhaps the centuries of greatest violence the West has ever known: the wars of religion were waged in the name of God; two million witches were burned and thousands of people were tortured by the Inquisition.

When religions become an end in themselves and are institutionalized as a form of power, whether sacred, social, cultural, or military (as in the former Papal States, which had an army and a bank), they lose contact with the source that keeps them alive, that is, spirituality.

Then, instead of charismatic and spiritual people, they produce bureaucrats of the sacred instead of pastors who take their place in the midst of the people, church authorities above the people and with their backs to them. They don't want the faithful to be creative but obedient; they don't foster maturity in faith but the infantilism that comes from subservience. The result is mediocrity, acceptance, an absence of prophets and martyrs, and a dumbing down of the word that should be inspiring new energy and new life.

With their dogmas, rites, and morality, religious institutions can become the tomb of the living God. In contrast, the founding fathers of spiritual paths—Buddha, Isaiah, Jesus Christ, St. Paul, Gandhi, Archbishop Hélder Câmara and Archbishop Óscar Romero (the latter from the sector of liberating Christianity)—are always deeply charismatic individuals who plunged into the Mystery in an extraordinary way and who bore witness to an encounter with Ultimate Reality, which we Christians call simply God. They were people who, through their encounter with the divine and the sacred, had their lives transformed by a deep inner change, in other words, by a spirituality from the deep source. This transformation matches the Dalai Lama's definition of spirituality: "everything that produces an inner change."

Cordial Reason: The Precondition for Spirituality

The basic question of spirituality is not knowing about God but feeling and experiencing God. To do this we have to go from the head to the heart. Analytic reason has to be complemented by sensitive or cordial reason. Blaise Pascal insisted long ago: "This is what faith is, God perceived by the heart, not by reason."

It is in cordial or sensitive reason that spirituality is practiced, because it is more than thinking about God; it is sensing God from the deepest dimension of ourselves. If we restrict ourselves solely to intellectual and analytic reason, we run the risk of making ourselves insensitive to the messages that come to us from all sides, from the grandeur of the universe and the delight of the plurality of forms of life on Earth. Pure reason alone without feeling makes us deaf to the cry of the oppressed and the groans of a creation subjected to the unrestrained desire to accumulate material goods. We enlarge the head and let the heart shrink in a sort of reverse lobotomy.

I have said this before, but it is worth repeating: it is the heart that houses the deep feelings of love, friendship, and compassion; it is the impulses of the heart that give us the courage to face obstacles and share the passion of our neighbor. Intellectual reason, which we cannot abandon if we are to deal with the problems of our complex societies, is only a few million years old, when our neocortical brain developed in us. Sensitive reason, or cordial reason, appeared over two hundred million years ago, when mammals appeared as part of the cosmogenic process. Mammals possess the limbic brain, the seat of affection, sensitivity, care, and love. When a mammal gives birth to its offspring, it surrounds them with affection, love, and care.

We forget that we belong to this lineage, that we are fundamentally creatures that feel, that are affected emotionally by others and have an emotional effect on others. We are endowed with *pathos*, which is more ancient than *logos*. The modern period made sensitive reason suspect because of its insistence on the objectivity of scientific inquiry. The new epistemology, however, has shown that this objectivity does not exist. All knowledge comes imbued with interests, as Jürgen Habermas has argued. The person who acquires knowledge approaches the object of knowledge with their ideas, visions of the world, and projections. As a result, subject and object are always interlocked, as quantum physics has demonstrated. Today it has become an urgent task to recover sensitive reason and strengthen the rights of the heart. The heart does not replace or diminish intellectual reason; it completes it and ensures that science is carried out with a conscience, more for the benefit of life than of the market and seeking financial profit.

Without sensitive or cordial reason we would have difficulty in perceiving God as a living experience, full of meaning, and one that leads us to have compassion for those who suffer, care for life, and maximize the biocapacity of Mother Earth, who has been wounded and crucified. Through the love created by cordial reason we commit ourselves to make our Common Home, Mother Earth, habitable and inclusive of all. There are many spiritual paths. We shall look at two, the Western and the Eastern.

The Two Paths of Spirituality, the Western and the Eastern

We going to leave the specifically Christian field for a moment and engage in a more basic reflection on spirituality, which underlies the two great paths followed by humankind in the East and in the West.

They are model spiritual paths, great in their inner richness, different and yet complementary. About these two types of experience sacred books and books of great wisdom have been written, methods of living the inner life have been devised, majestic places, visited by countless followers, have been constructed where the spiritual and religious life can be lived.

What I am going to say will be extremely schematic, because I will be concentrating only on the original intuition of each of these two spiritual paths. The two basic affirmations are:

1. There exists the path of personal communion with God that includes everything—the Western path.
2. There exists the path of communion with the whole, which includes God—the Eastern path.

East and West come together and offer us the possibility of a comprehensive and totalizing experience of God, the Divine, or the Mystery.

To begin with we shall suspend any value judgment about these two paths and not ask, as many people mistakenly do, which is better, more up-to-date, or more in accord with God's will.

Since we have talked about the Dalai Lama several times, allow me to reveal part of a conversation I had with him years ago, which will help us to understand the issue I am going to address. In a break between sessions of a roundtable on religion and peace between peoples, in Berlin, in which we were both taking part, I asked him in my poor English, mischievously but with real theological interest: "Holiness, which religion is the best?" I expected him to say: "Tibetan Buddhism" or "the Eastern religions. They are much older than Christianity." He paused for a moment, smiled, looked me straight in the eye, which took me back a little, because I realized that my question had a mischievous side, and said: "The best religion is the one that makes you better." To escape my confusion at such a wise answer, I asked another question: "What makes me better?" And he replied:

> The one that makes you more compassionate [and here I sensed the Tibetan, Buddhist, Taoist resonance of his reply], the one that makes you more sensitive, more detached, more loving, more humanitarian, more responsible . . . The religion that is able to do that to you is the best religion.

I was silent in admiration, and ever since I have been thinking about his wise and irrefutable answer.

So we cannot assert, as is done currently at some of the highest and most closed levels of some conservatively inclined ecclesiastical authorities, that Christianity on its own possesses the invincible and unique arsenal of the means of salvation, doesn't need the help of other religions, and is the only path willed by God for reaching him.

As well as being arrogant, this assertion is theologically wrong, because the whole ocean of God's grace and love doesn't fit into our container, and all the greatness of God is not exhausted by our talk. In the light of what the Dalai Lama said, each of us is challenged to ask: What is my path? Where does my humanity flower best? Where can I have a more radical encounter with God and show him my reverence? Where can I become a creature that radiates, is able, together with others, to grow in humanity, to become more forgiving, to be more able to include others, so that no one is excluded from our world, from our community, from our world?

The Western Path of Spirituality

Let us briefly look at the Western path. It has been fundamentally marked by the Judeo-Christian experience, which is centered on the encounter with God, a God who reveals himself and says his name, Yahweh, which means: "I am the one who is fully here and who walks with you, accompanies you, and establishes a dialogue with you."

A relationship with God is personal and based on dialogue. It is an "I-Thou" encounter between unequal partners, who are able, however, through openness, friendship, and love, to establish communions and inaugurate an alliance. Dialogue is fundamental, as was demonstrated by the philosophers of existential encounter, such as Martin Buber.

In anthropological terms, it is in this I-Thou dialogue that human identity is formed. It is on the basis of the Thou that we discover our own I. It is not a merely intellectual encounter with a God who would fit only in our heads. It is fundamentally an experience of love, in which we feel wrapped in the divine reality. It is a total encounter, because it moves our inner selves, making us fall on our knees, like Moses or St. Peter, weeping and giving praise.

We dialogue lovingly with God and want to know him better, in a true process of falling in love. When we fall in love with a person, everything about them becomes interesting: where they were born, what their family is like, where they were educated, what they like. Every detail takes on importance and becomes sacramental, because it is in this encounter that we grow, go into ecstasy, and have the experience of the most radical openness to the other, to the point of being willing to sacrifice everything for them, unite our fate with theirs, and, ultimately, merge with them. In this experience we feel radically human and are unable to think of happiness or eternity except as an infinite extension of this experience of full meaning.

Because we want to be united with the person we love, we change our habits, accept to give up all sorts of things; we don't count the time or measure the difficulties, provided that we find them. It was in this sort of experience that the West had its encounter with God, an encounter of growing love, which leads us to want to understand God more and more, in order to love God more and more, unceasingly.

Anyone who reads the great Christian mystics like St. John of the Cross (1542–1591), St. Teresa of Avila (1515–1582), or Meister Eckhart (1260–1328) comes into contact with this experience of love. Only someone who had a radical meeting with God in love could write, as St. John of the Cross does in his *Spiritual Canticle*:

> Reveal Your presence,
> And let the vision and Your beauty kill me.
> Behold, the malady
> Of love is incurable
> Except in Your presence and before Your face.
>
> (Stanza 11)[1]

Or St. Teresa of Avila in *Aspirations to Eternal Life*:

> Now I live outside myself
> Because I am dying of love;
> Because I live in the Lord,
> Who wanted me for himself.
> When I gave him my heart

---

1. *A Spiritual Canticle of the Soul and the Bridegroom Christ* (Grand Rapids, MI: Christian Classics Ethereal Library, 2007), https://www.ccel.org/ccel/john_cross/canticle.html, p. 54.

I put this label on it:
I am dying because I am not dying.
[Verse 1]

Returning to St. John of the Cross, we see the permanent search for love that surrenders itself and retires:

Shepherds, as you go up
Further, through the pastures to the hilltop,
If by chance you see
The one I most desire,
Tell him I am sick, suffering and dying.
[*Love Songs between the Soul and God*, verse 2]

Such expressions are possible only on the assumption of a mystic I-Thou relationship, an encounter in which the encounter can always fail, in which, as much as one knows and loves the person, their mystery is never totally unveiled. They veil themselves and reveal themselves, come forward and go back. This makes it a magical encounter, fascinating, full of care and reverence, in which limits have to be respected because the slightest movement can cloud the whole experience of encounter.

As everything is linked umbilically to God, through him we encounter the whole. God is mirrored in the universe and penetrates into the heart of each thing; the universe and each thing meet in God. To express this mutual presence, Christian theology created the expression "panentheism," which means God is in all things. It is not pantheism, which is when everything without distinction is in God.

God and the world retain their difference, since one is creator and the other created. But they interpenetrate each other and are present to each other. God is present in all things and vice versa, without any distance. God is in the depths of our hearts, and therefore we are not far from him. In him we live and move and have our being, as St. Paul reminded his audience at the Areopagus in Athens (Acts 17:28). We are in God as we are in the air we breathe, and God is in us as the air in our lungs keeps us alive.

That is what Teilhard de Chardin, the extraordinary twentieth-century Jesuit and palaeontologist, called the "divine milieu": we are in God, we never leave God, or go to God because *we are always in God.*

Faith's task is to discover this God who is present in all things, but hidden under a thousand signs. The universe is a huge sacrament; matter is sacred, and nature is spiritual. Why? Because it is God's temple. God is in everything and everything is in God, everything is reflected in God. The universe is not a matter of indifference to God; it is in God's heart and belongs to the realm of the Trinity.

Saint Francis of Assisi, in his cosmic mysticism, lived emotionally this spirituality of God in the whole and the whole in God. That is why he universalized the idea of being children of God and brothers and sisters to all creatures, Brother Sun, Sister Moon, Sister Water, and Brother Fire, not forgetting Brother Body and Sister Death.

I find deeply consoling something that Pope St. John Paul II often said, that we are born out of a loving act of God and are anchored in the Father's heart.

Turned into a doctrine, this statement would be one among many, but if we transform it into a movement of the heart, we will have an experience of spirituality and profound liberation. Why should we be afraid if God is for us? Why should we be afraid if we are in God's hands? Why do our hearts thrill if they are inhabited by the Most High?

Life becomes light, is transformed into enchantment and poetry because, as in the poems of St. John of the Cross or St. Francis's Canticle to Brother Sun, everything speaks to us of God. Sheep, meadows, air, water, fire, clouds, the starry sky are all some of the signs of greeting from God in everything that surrounds us.

Pope Francis has beautiful words on this in his encyclical *Laudato Si'*: "Everything is related, and we human beings are united . . . in fond affection with Brother Sun, Sister Moon, Brother River and Mother Earth" (§92).

The experience of faith transfigures our world and makes it a sacrament, despite all the contradictions that never go away. But the contradictions are not able to erase the signs left by Love. Our challenge is, therefore, discovering how to move from the head, the site of doctrine about God, to the heart, where the living reality of God is to be found. *God is in our hearts.*

The author of 1 John puts this in an extremely felicitous way: "That which was from the beginning, which we have heard, which we have seen with our eyes, which we have looked upon and touched with our hands, concerning the word of life . . . we proclaim also to you" (1 John 1:1). It is felt experience, heard, seen, touched. Western spirituality had that spiritual experience that enabled it to synthesize all reality in God.

This faith has to be vigorous to be able to see God, really, in all things, even the most contradictory. Perhaps we cannot explain the presence of this divine presence within the reality of negativity, as much as we try to unravel the mystery. In the end, surely we have to conclude with St. Thomas Aquinas in his Treatise on Evil: "We do not understand evil, but we believe that God is so powerful that he can bring good out of evil, because if that were not the case, God would not be omnipotent."

It is only through this living faith that we can sing, as the Catholic liturgy does at the Easter Vigil, "O happy fault," through which we experience God's mercy on human smallness, and which makes us realize that we are never far from God or out of touch with God. And it is on the basis of this experience of encounter that the many spiritual families were created that bear witness to God in the whole and the whole in God, in a deep communion and loving inter-retro-connection, whether it is the Sufi mysticism of Rumi or Ibn Arabi or the Christian mysticism of St. Francis of Assisi, St. John of the Cross, or Teilhard de Chardin. It is the spiritual path of the West.

The Eastern Path of Spirituality

The East took a different path, also one of grandeur and even more ancient than our Western one.

The first experience a person who follows the Eastern path of spirituality, possibly a monk, has is one of totality, in other words, of the unity of reality. Things are not placed side by side, juxtaposed, but are all symphonic, interlinked. There is a great unity, but a complex unity, composed of different levels, many different creatures, all connected and linked together. This produces a deep, intense dynamism.

When the yoga master asks, "Who are you?," he or she spreads their arms, points to the universe, and says: "You are all this. We are this whole reality, we are part and parcel of the whole, we are the whole."

Our sense of rootlessness and the human drama is feeling part of, and losing the memory of being part of, the whole; it is feeling oneself a living link and forgetting that this link is part of a single chain of life. How do we combine our consciousness, which is singular and personal, with this totality?

The whole Eastern quest consists in constructing a path that leads to an experience of totality. It is, as they say, a search for an experience of nonduality. This means feeling oneself a stone, a plant, an animal, a star, in a word—feeling oneself the universe.

The Dalai Lama himself tells that once great American scientists took him to a nuclear research center and showed him on a receiver the signs electrons leave, because no one can see atoms, still less an electron, only the traces of its passage. The Dalai Lama smiled and said: "While I was still a boy, I saw all the atoms, all the electrons, all the protons; I saw the most distant stars, because I was initiated into communion with all things."

The electron, therefore, is not out there, the electron is here within us—the Dalai Lama himself identified with it. Buddhism initiates people into the Tao that is found in all things. Each thing possesses its particular Tao. By uniting ourselves with the Tao of all things, we also unite with ourselves and we dive into the whole. In this connection, a short poem by Chuang-tzu, translated by Thomas Merton in his book *The Way of Chuang Tzu*, reflects this path. One of Chuang-tzu's disciples asks, "Show me where the Tao is found." Chuang-tzu replies, "There is no where it is not to be found." When the disciple asks for some definite place, Chuang-tzu points to the ant, the weeds, a piece of tile, and finally a turd, which left the disciple silent. But Chuang continued:

> None of your questions
> Are to the point. They are like the questions
> Of inspectors in the market,
> Testing the weight of pigs
> By prodding them in their thinnest parts.
> Why look for Tao by going "down the scale of being"
> As if that which we call "least"
> Had less of Tao?
> Tao is great in all things,
> Complete in all, Universal in all,
> Whole in all. These three aspects
> Are distinct. But the Reality is One.

As we see, the Tao pervades everything and makes diversity flow into the One. How can we have the experience of the One which is the Whole?

One of the first exercises performed in Eastern mysticism, whether in the Yoga path or the Tao path, is the lightstream exercise, which many people in the West also know and practice. You imagine a light coming from the center of the universe and falling on your head. This light is taken in and gradually takes over the body, from its center. It occupies your whole being, expands still further and includes the walls of your room, the trees, the mountains, the sea, and extends to the whole universe, until you feel completely one with the whole. This is the practice of an experience of non-duality. We are all this.

Whereas the spiritual path of the East seeks the inner depths of the human being, our Western path seeks the out-side. One way is outward-directed, seeking to conquer exter-nal space, to reach the furthest limits, to demand the infinity of the sky above our heads. The other is inward-directed, traveling along the meanders of our desires, the depth of our intentions, toward our own heart.

As one of the Sri Lankan Buddhist mystics said, "The inner path is as dangerous as the outward path." It is as dan-gerous as going to the moon, to Mars, or the most distant galaxies, because we run the risk of making a mistake, get-ting lost, and even sinking and dying.

Eastern mysticism seeks to create an inner center with such strength and energy that it turns all reality around it into a satellite, re-creating the perception of totality. And we move around in this totality as we do in our own homes, with complete calm, with no fear, because nothing can threaten us. Everything is wrapped around this powerful center cre-ated by meditation, by detachment, by an extremely coher-ent ethical path.

These two experiences opened up the historical spiritual paths of Buddhism, Hinduism, and Taoism in China, Japan, and Korea. They are cultural ways of translating that source experience and have produced, as in the West, many spiritual and religious institutions. Behind each of them is a vigorous spiritual experience.

It would also be interesting to identify the spiritual experience active behind the Afro-Brazilian religions and in particular the specifically Brazilian one, Umbanda, founded by Zélio Fernandino de Moraes in Niterói, Rio de Janeiro, in 1908. These religions have thousands of followers in Brazil, the rest of Latin America, and particularly in Africa.

These religions give a deeply ecological experience, centered on the reality of *axé*, which corresponds approximately to the Qi for Easterners or the Holy Spirit in the Judeo-Christian tradition: a cosmic energy that pervades the whole universe and impregnates the whole of reality, but concentrated in human beings, essentially more in women than men, which makes every reality radiant and alive.

The *exu* in Afro-Brazilian religions is not a demon we have to drive out but the special bearer of *axé*, universal energy. *Axé* acts within us as a radiating force, as an openness to capture more energies and put them at the services of others. But it would take us a long time to follow this topic, if we were to do justice to millions of Black men and women who belong to Afro-Brazilian religions. This brief summary will have to do.

In this context we might recall the dialogue the great psychoanalyst C. G. Jung had in 1924–1925 with Ochwiay Biano, a member of the Pueblo indigenous tribe in New Mexico. Biano thought that white people were mad.

"I asked him why he thought the whites were all mad. 'They say that they think with their heads,' he replied. 'Why of course. What do you think with?' I asked him in surprise. 'We think here,' he said, indicating his heart" (C. G. Jung, *Memories, Dreams, Reflections*, p. 300).

This encounter transformed Jung's thinking. He realized that the Europeans had conquered the world with their heads but had lost the capacity to think with the heart and live through the soul (see Anthony Stevens, *On Jung*). Fundamentally they had lost the dimension of spirituality.

The paths of East and West are not in opposition but complementary. Both aim fundamentally at creating in us what we so much seek, a center from which everything connects and reconnects and allows us to live in totality. It matters little what we call this center, but it corresponds to what is meant by God, Tao, and Olorum. This center is in us, but it also overflows us. It is the living inner Mystery of our lives and of the universe.

Mysticism as the Highest Form of Spirituality

Spirituality is about experience, not doctrine, not dogmas, not rites, not liturgical celebrations, which are simply institutional paths that can help us in spirituality but are subsequent to it. They emerged from spirituality; they may contain spirituality, but they are not spirituality. They are piped water, not the spring of sparkling water.

It is not easy to maintain the dialectic between spirituality and religion. Very often we reach a true spiritual experience only by dismantling the religious edifice, rather as goldminers break up the rock that hides the precious ore.

A model for this process is the Book of Job. There are forty-two chapters in which Job, step by step, deconstructs religion with its doctrines, its justice, and its pretensions. Job starts by disputing with his wife, with his four friends, then with everyone who approaches him, and finally faces God himself. And God accepts the challenge: "Shall a faultfinder contend with the Almighty? He who argues with God, let him answer it" (Job 40:2).

This is Job's supreme arrogance, our supreme dignity. We are not wasting time in petty quarrels; it is God himself that we are facing. The psalms show this well. They are full of lamentations, even curses, alongside many expressions of praise and thanksgiving. But in all this we have the experience of the sacred, religious experience, spiritual experience. God accepts the confrontation and challenges Job to dialogue with him: "Where were you when I laid the foundation of the earth? . . . Have you commanded the morning since your days began, and caused the dawn to know its place? . . . Do you give the horse his might? . . . Is it at your command that the eagle mounts up and makes his nest on high?" Job becomes increasingly small and finally confesses: "Behold, I am of small account; what shall I answer thee? I lay my hand on my mouth. . . . I know that thou canst do all things, and that no purpose of thine can be thwarted" (Job 38–42).

Finally Job gives in. He no longer sticks to the religious speeches that led him to doubts and endless disputes. Now he has a spiritual experience that reconciles everything. He puts it beautifully: "I had heard of thee by the hearing of the ear, but now my eye sees thee; therefore I despise myself, and repent in dust and ashes" (Job 42:5–6).

We are all, in a way, the biblical Job. We are no longer content with people talking about God; we are tired of theologies, books, encyclicals, and homilies. We want to find people who talk in God's way, who talk to God. Only then will we have a rest from all our interminable questions and cuddle up to God himself.

Allow me to digress. Once I went to preach a retreat for a group of bishops, and I asked each of them to say how they prayed. One after the other, they made a speech about prayer. When it was Pedro Casaldáliga's turn, that great pastor, prophet, and mystic uttered a beautiful prayer. Instead of talking about prayer, he prayed:

God, Father and Mother of goodness, of all the things in the universe: look on our world, at the open wounds, at the blood flowing from our Pachamama, Mother Earth, and from the bodies of our brothers and sisters oppressed by the large landowners and economic exploitation. Help us to revive the Earth and build a society where there is room for all, with new hearts, new men and women. Only then, Lord, can we praise you together for our whole lives, now and forever.

This spiritual pastor, a poet and mystic like St. John of the Cross, did not lecture on doctrines about prayer or about God; he talked to God. It is for people like that that we hunger and thirst. When they appear, they attract crowds of followers because they are seminal. They function like seeds that enrich the ground, awaken in us the spiritual dimension, that dimension of depth that surpasses our immediate interests—work, life, happiness—the dimension that goes beyond the competition that our capitalist society forces on to us, beyond the daily struggle for bread and beauty.

Spirituality lives off gratuitousness and availability; it lives off the capacity for tenderness and compassion, lives off honesty in the face of reality and by listening to the message that constantly comes from that reality. It breaks the relationship of possessing things and establishes a relationship of communion with them. Rather than using, it contemplates.

In Rio de Janeiro, when we are facing the sea and the huge waves beside the Avenida Niemeyer, we don't just see the sea, we see majesty and power. Or when we are high up by the statue of Christ on Corcovado, we see beauty rather than stone. Stone, sea, and all of nature have messages; they speak to us; and, if we are spiritual, we can listen to them. When we bend over a newborn baby, we are filled with tenderness; we are dazzled at the mystery of life, the shining eyes. And when we meet a person whose wisdom does not depend on academic education, we are filled with reverence, respect, and want to listen to them carefully.

So developing our spirituality means developing our capacity for contemplation, for listening to the messages and values that impregnate the world around us. This is the point of entry for mysticism, the highest form of spirituality. Mystics feel in such deep communion with God that they feel united to God—in the words of St. John of the Cross, "the beloved transformed into the lover" or "being God through participation."

Mystics are so united to God that they see God in all things and feel that they are in the palm of God's hand. The lines of the English poet and mystic William Blake (1757–1837), who saw God in everything:

> To see a World in a Grain of Sand
> And a Heaven in a Wild Flower
> Hold Infinity in the palm of your hand
> And Eternity in an hour.

This is evidence of a mystical experience. It is not about knowing God but about feeling God in all things

"We Are a Mystical Quality of the Earth"

Finally, to round off these reflections on spirituality in its two basic forms, the Western and the Eastern, what better way than with some words from the father of North American ecotheology, Thomas Berry? He is a theologian and cultural anthropologist and worked with the great cosmologist Brian Swimme, with whom he wrote what is perhaps the best text on the history of the universe, which combines science and spirituality, *The Universe Story*. Berry says:

> We must feel that we are supported by the same power that brought the Earth into being, that power that spun the galaxies into space, that lit the sun and brought the moon into its orbit. That is the power by which living forms grew up out of the Earth and came to a special mode of human consciousness in the human. . . . By definition, we are that reality in whom the entire Earth comes to a special mode of reflexive consciousness. We

are ourselves a mystical quality of the Earth, a unifying principle, an integration of the various polarities of the material and the spiritual, the physical and the psychic, the natural and the artistic, the intuitive and the scientific. . . . We are the unity in which all these inhere. . . . We live immersed in a sea of energy beyond all comprehension. But this energy, in an ultimate sense, is ours, not by domination but by invocation. (*The Great Work: Our Way into the Future* [New York: Bell Tower, 1999], pp. 174–75)

This Energy is the Creator Spirit that acts in cosmogenesis, anthropogenesis, and in our hearts. Spirituality is watched over by this powerful and loving Energy. Opening ourselves generously to it is living the deep dimension of our existence. The result is great peace and serenity, like that of someone who feels in their soul that they are in God's hand.

This spirituality is a mode of being, a basic attitude to be lived in each moment and in all circumstances. Even while performing the daily domestic tasks, working in a factory, traveling by car, talking to friends, enjoying intimacy with the person we love, the person who made space for depth and spirituality is centered, serene, and radiates peace. They sprinkle vitality and enthusiasm (which comes from a Greek word for having a god inside oneself) because they are inhabited by God. That God is Love, which, as the poet Dante said, moves the heaven and all the stars—and I would add, our own hearts.

A Minimal Spirituality of Mother Earth

Spirituality, or the life of the spirit, emerges in us when we move from ideas to the heart, from doctrines to experience. It is one thing to say, "Earth is our mother," and have simply a new concept about the planet. It is another thing to feel inwardly and with the whole of our being that Earth is our mother.

When we breathe we feel that it is our Mother who gives us the strength to live. When we eat, we realize, in an existential experience, the generosity of our Mother, who offers us all that we need, which we eat with pleasure, especially when we eat with others, all seated at the table like the big family gathered together. When, after a day's work, she offers us the relaxing rest of a bed. When we wake up, we give thanks for another day of life. When we leave for work, it is she who gives us the energy to produce and the enthusiasm to keep going back to the daily grind.

When we meet our wife or husband with the children, grandchildren, and relatives, we see vividly how our Mother, through us, has generated life and clasped us to her bosom. When we slowly climb the mountain of life and then come down toward old age, we feel that she is accompanying us and giving us wise lessons about our limitations. When we raise our minds to God, she prompts us to give thanks, to give praise and spiritual worship. And finally, when we have run our course, it is she who reveals to us that dying is being born anew to God and that we have been called by God to live eternally with God in a house prepared for us by God from all eternity.

If life can come into being in a context of care, it is through permanent care, all the time it exists on the face of the Earth, that life persists, reproduces, and co-evolves. Just as it is part of the essence of human beings and of all reality, care can serve as a minimal consensus on which we can base a planetary ethics, an ethics that all can understand and practice.

This ethics is strengthened by a spiritual sense of life that doesn't let life become a limiting superego or a mere sterile legalism. On the contrary, it creates in us an inner joy and peace that only spirituality can give.

The base of this ethics is a serene culture of peace that produces calm and exorcizes all fears because we are welcomed by the generous Mother and by God, who, in his action in history, showed that he is a Father and Mother of infinite tenderness and goodness.

The Black Brazilian poet and singer Milton Nascimento has a song that contains the line, "We have to care for the shoot for life to give us flower and fruit." This applies to the Earth and all its ecosystems: in the words of the Earth Charter, we have to "care for the community of life with understanding, compassion, and love," which means caring for the Earth understood as Gaia, *Magna Mater*, Common Home, Pachamama, as she is known by the Andean peoples, so that she can maintain her vitality, integrity, and beauty.

Earth and humankind: together we are a single unit, as the astronauts saw with such emotion when they looked at the Earth from space. Only care will guarantee the sustainability of the Earth system with all the creatures of the community of life, among whom are human beings, one more link in this immense chain of life, but with a unique responsibility, that of being the guardian and caretaker of the inheritance that God, through the cosmogenic process, entrusted to us.

The mission of humankind is to be a gardener, as described in the second chapter of the book of Genesis, and the gardener's job is to care for the Garden of Eden, make it fruitful and beautiful. The Earth Charter and Pope Francis have awakened us, at the right time, for our mission, which is essential and urgent.

I would like to conclude this book with a hymn of praise to Mother Earth:

Earth, Common Home, Our Mother, and God's Body

Earth, my beloved, Great Mother and Common Home: You have been coming to birth slowly for millions and millions of years, pregnant with creative energies.

Your body, made of cosmic dust, was a seed in the womb of the great red stars, which later exploded, launching you into limitless space.

You came and nested, like an embryo in the bosom of an ancestral star, within the Milky Way, which later became a supernova. This too fell victim to such splendor.

And then you stopped in the welcoming bosom of a nebula, where, now a young woman, you wandered around looking for a home. And the nebula became denser and turned into a Sun, glorious in light and heat.

This Sun fell in love with you, pulled you to him and wanted you in his orbit, along with Mars, Mercury, Venus, and other planets. And he married you. From your marriage to the Sun were born sons and daughters, fruits of your boundless fertility, from the tiniest bacteria, viruses, and fungi to the bigger and more complex living creatures, such as the dinosaurs. And as a noble expression of the history of life, you bore us, men and women.

Through us, beloved Earth, you feel, think, love, speak, and venerate. And you continue growing, as an adult, within the universe toward the bosom of the Father-and-Mother God of infinite tenderness. From this God we came and to this God we shall return with a lack that only this God can fill. O God, Father and Mother of goodness, we want to submerge in you and be one with you forever together with Mother Earth.

And now, beloved Earth, I perform the action Jesus performed in the power of his Spirit. Like him, filled with spiritual power, I take you in my impure hands and pronounce over you the sacred words the universe was hiding and which you longed to hear: "*Hoc est enim corpus meum*: This is my Body. *Hic est sanguis meus*. This is my blood." And then I felt it: what was Earth was transformed into Paradise, and what was human life was transfigured into divine life. What was bread became God's body, and what was wine became sacred blood.

Finally, Earth, with your sons and daughters, you came to God. You became God by participation. At home, at last.

Do this in memory of me. Therefore, from time immemorial, I obey the Lord's command. I pronounce the essential word over you, beloved Mother Earth, and over the whole universe. And with the universe and with you we feel ourselves the Body of God, in the full splendor of God's glory.

After this, there is nothing more to say. We keep a reverent silence and silent reverence.

Selection of Works by Leonardo Boff

Here are listed works available in English translation on themes treated in the present volume. Following the title is the year of original publication.

Becoming New: Finding God within Us and in Creation, with Anselm Grün (2017) (Maryknoll, NY: Orbis Books, 2019).

Christianity in a Nutshell (2011) (Maryknoll, NY: Orbis Books, 2013).

Church: Charism and Power (1981) (New York: Crossroad, 1985).

Come, Holy Spirit: Inner Fire, Giver of Life & Comforter of the Poor (2013) (Maryknoll, NY: Orbis Books, 2015).

Cry of the Earth, Cry of the Poor (1995) (Maryknoll, NY: Orbis Books, 1997).

Ecclesiogenesis: The Base Communities Reinvent the Church (1977) (Maryknoll, NY: Orbis Books, 1986).

Ecology & Liberation: A New Paradigm (1993) (Maryknoll, NY: Orbis Books, 1995).

Essential Care: An Ethics of Human Nature (Waco, TX: Baylor University, 2008).

Faith on the Edge: Religion and Marginalized Existence (1978, 1980) (Maryknoll, NY: Orbis Books, 1991).

The Following of Jesus: A Reply to The Imitation of Christ (2016) (Maryknoll, NY: Orbis Books, 2019).

Francis of Assisi: A Model for Human Liberation (1981) (Maryknoll, NY: Orbis Books, 2006).

Francis of Rome, Francis of Assisi: A New Springtime for the Church (2013) (Maryknoll, NY: Orbis Books, 2014).

Global Civilization: Challenges to Society and Christianity (2003) (New York: Routledge, 2005).

Holy Trinity, Perfect Community (1988) (Maryknoll, NY: Orbis Books, 2000).

Introducing Liberation Theology, with Clodovis Boff (1986) (Maryknoll, NY: Orbis Books, 1987).

Jesus Christ Liberator: A Critical Christology for Our Time (1972) (Maryknoll, NY: Orbis Books, 1978).

Liberating Grace (1976) (Maryknoll, NY: Orbis Books, 1979).

The Lord Is My Shepherd: Divine Consolation in Times of Abandonment (2004) (Maryknoll, NY: Orbis Books, 2006).

Maternal Face of God: The Feminine and Its Religious Expressions (1979) (New York: Harper & Row, 1987).

New Evangelization: Good News to the Poor (1990) (Maryknoll, NY: Orbis Books, 1991).

Passion of Christ, Passion of the World (1977) (Maryknoll, NY: Orbis Books, 1987).

The Path to Hope: Fragments from a Theologian's Journey (1991) (Maryknoll, NY: Orbis Books, 1993).

The Prayer of St. Francis: A Message of Peace for the World Today (1999) (Maryknoll, NY: Orbis Books, 2001).

Praying with Jesus and Mary: Our Father, Hail Mary (1979, 1980) (Maryknoll, NY: Orbis Books, 2005).

Saint Joseph: The Father of God in a Fatherless Society (Eugene, OR: Cascade Books, 2009).

Salvation and Liberation: In Search of a Balance between Faith and Politics, with Clodovis Boff (1979) (Maryknoll, NY: Orbis Books, 1984).

The Tao of Liberation: Exploring the Ecology of Transformation, with Mark Hathaway (Maryknoll, NY: Orbis Books, 2009).

Toward an Eco-Spirituality (2014) (New York: Crossroad: 2015).

Trinity and Society (1986) (Maryknoll, NY: Orbis Books, 1988).

Way of the Cross, Way of Justice (1978) (Maryknoll, NY: Orbis Books, 1980).

When Theology Listens to the Poor (New York: Harper & Row, 1988).